MEETING,
and EXCEEDING
EXPECTATIONS

A Guide to Successful Nonprofit Board Meetings

SECOND EDITION

Outi Flynn

BOARDSOURCE®
Building Effective Nonprofit Boards

Library of Congress Cataloging-in-Publication Data

Flynn, Outi

   Meeting, and exceeding expectations : a guide to successful nonprofit board
meetings / Outi Flynn. -- 2nd ed.

      p. cm. --

   Prev. ed. published in 2004 under title: Meet smarter : a guide to better nonprofit
board meeting.

   Includes bibliographical references and index.

   ISBN 1-58686-115-8 (alk. paper)

1. Corporate meetings--Handbooks, manuals, etc. 2. Business meetings--
Handbooks, manuals, etc. 3. Boards of directors--Handbooks, manuals, etc. 4.
Chief executive officers--Handbooks, manuals, etc. 5. Parliamentary practice--
Handbooks, manuals, etc. 6. Nonprofit organizations--Management--Handbooks,
manuals, etc. I. Flynn, Outi. Meet smarter : a guide to better nonprofit board
meeting. II. Title.

              HD2743.F57 2009
              658.4'56--dc22   2009024225

© 2009 BoardSource.
First Printing, July 2009
ISBN 1-58686-115-8 (alk. paper)

Published by BoardSource
750 9th Street, NW, Suite 650
Washington, DC 20001-2521

BOARDSOURCE®
Building Effective Nonprofit Boards

BoardSource is dedicated to advancing the public good by building exceptional nonprofit boards and inspiring board service.

BoardSource was established in 1988 by the Association of Governing Boards of Universities and Colleges (AGB) and Independent Sector (IS). Prior to this, in the early 1980s, the two organizations had conducted a survey and found that although 30 percent of respondents believed they were doing a good job of board education and training, the rest of the respondents reported little, if any, activity in strengthening governance. As a result, AGB and IS proposed the creation of a new organization whose mission would be to increase the effectiveness of nonprofit boards.

With a lead grant from the Kellogg Foundation and funding from five other donors, BoardSource opened its doors in 1988 as the National Center for Nonprofit Boards with a staff of three and an operating budget of $385,000. On January 1, 2002, BoardSource took on its new name and identity. These changes were the culmination of an extensive process of understanding how we were perceived, what our audiences wanted, and how we could best meet the needs of nonprofit organizations.

Today, BoardSource is the premier voice of nonprofit governance. Its highly acclaimed products, programs, and services mobilize boards so that organizations fulfill their missions, achieve their goals, increase their impact, and extend their influence. BoardSource is a 501(c)(3) organization.

BoardSource provides

- resources to nonprofit leaders through workshops, training, and an extensive Web site (www.boardsource.org)

- governance consultants who work directly with nonprofit leaders to design specialized solutions to meet an organization's needs

- the world's largest, most comprehensive selection of material on nonprofit governance, including a large selection of books and CD-ROMs

- an annual conference that brings together approximately 900 governance experts, board members, and chief executives and senior staff from around the world

For more information, please visit our Web site at www.boardsource.org, e-mail us at mail@boardsource.org, or call us at 800-883-6262.

Have You Used These BoardSource Resources?

THE GOVERNANCE SERIES

1. *Ten Basic Responsibilities of Nonprofit Boards, Second Edition*
2. *Legal Responsibilities of Nonprofit Boards, Second Edition*
3. *Financial Responsibilities of Nonprofit Boards, Second Edition*
4. *Fundraising Responsibilities of Nonprofit Boards, Second Edition*
5. *The Nonprofit Board's Role in Mission, Planning, and Evaluation, Second Edition*
6. *Structures and Practices of Nonprofit Boards, Second Edition*

BOOKS

The Board Chair Handbook, Second Edition

Getting the Best from Your Board: An Executive's Guide to a Successful Partnership

Understanding Nonprofit Financial Statements, Third Edition

Taming the Troublesome Board Member

The Nonprofit Board Answer Book: A Practical Guide for Board Members and Chief Executives, Second Edition

The Board Building Cycle: Nine Steps to Finding, Recruiting, and Engaging Nonprofit Board Members, Second Edition

Navigating the Organizational Lifecycle: A Capacity-Building Guide for Nonprofit Leaders

The Nonprofit Dashboard: A Tool for Tracking Progress

Financial Committees

The Nonprofit Legal Landscape

The Nonprofit Board's Guide to Bylaws

Managing Conflicts of Interest: A Primer for Nonprofit Boards, Second Edition

The Nonprofit Policy Sampler, Second Edition

Chief Executive Transitions: How to Hire and Support a Nonprofit CEO

Chief Executive Succession Planning: The Board's Role in Securing Your Organization's Future

Assessment of the Chief Executive

Moving Beyond Founder's Syndrome to Nonprofit Success

The Source: Twelve Principles of Governance That Power Exceptional Boards

Exceptional Board Practices: The Source in Action

Fearless Fundraising for Nonprofit Boards, Second Edition

Driving Strategic Planning: A Nonprofit Executive's Guide

Culture of Inquiry: Healthy Debate in the Boardroom

Who's Minding the Money?: An Investment Guide for Nonprofit Board Members

DVDs

Meeting the Challenge: An Orientation to Nonprofit Board Service

Speaking of Money: A Guide to Fundraising for Nonprofit Board Members

ONLINE ASSESSMENTS

Board Self-Assessment

Assessment of the Chief Executive

Executive Search — Needs Assessment

For an up-to-date list of publications and information about current prices, membership, and other services, please call BoardSource at 800-883-6262 or visit our Web site at www.boardsource.org. For consulting services, please email us at consulting@boardsource.org or call 877-892-6293.

CONTENTS

INTRODUCTION

Q **Our board meets only twice a year. Is that really enough?**

A Legally, you are probably compliant, but remember, the law does not stipulate what you should do; it simply states the minimum legal requirement for your board. By asking the question, you are obviously wondering whether your board is on top of all it has to accomplish. If a meeting is the only place where the board can make decisions, it must be extremely organized and busy between meetings. It takes time to research and prepare for issues, anticipate the unexpected, and take care of the board's own needs and education. Very few boards can manage these expectations and feel confident that it is fulfilling all of its fiduciary duties in two yearly meetings. This might be a good question for your board to discuss and answer at its next meeting.

Every incorporated nonprofit is required to have a board. As there are no owners in a nonprofit organization — not counting the stakeholders and the constituencies as the symbolic owners — the board acts in the capacity of an owner that is legally accountable for what happens in the organization. Groups with such a responsibility must find a setting, i.e., a board meeting, to exercise that duty.

A board cannot perform without meeting. A meeting is the place for a board to make decisions, a place where individual board members "fuse" into the group that is responsible and liable for the organization. A meeting is where the board performs its role as the policy maker, sets the direction for the organization, defines and follows its own ethical guidelines, oversees the operations, and takes care of its own well-being. Together, individuals act as the board. Individually, members cannot make organizational decisions, but they can perform certain tasks on behalf of the board outside of the meeting room, such as fundraising, advocacy, or acting as ambassadors in the community.

ATTENDANCE IS REQUIRED

The board's role is to advance the mission of the nonprofit organization it governs. All decisions and actions ultimately are supposed to reflect and support that mission. Keeping the mission front and center in the minds of the decision makers ensures that the purpose of the organization is not overlooked.

Meeting attendance is not optional. It is a duty that comes with board service. Individual board members are bound by their duty of care, a legal obligation that defines the thoughtfulness and consideration that they must exercise in their role as the guardians of the organization. In practice, this means that a board member comes prepared to meetings, asks probing questions, pays attention, and makes decisions according to his or her best judgment. Coming prepared means that the member is familiar with the agenda, has read the board book, and has completed any assignments from the previous meeting.

Generally, all of the board's activities cannot be accomplished in a meeting that lasts only a few hours, so individuals, task forces, and committees carry out decisions made in the boardroom or prepare work for the full board to act on at the next meeting. All this action culminates in a masterfully conducted board meeting where every minute is spent on issues that advance the mission of the organization. This may sound idealistic, but with a solid objective as a guide, any board can improve its performance and members leave the meeting with a sense of real accomplishment and personal satisfaction.

A board meeting also serves the role of gathering together the decision makers and allowing them to interact in a manner that triggers productive communication and teamwork. During a board meeting, members get to know their peers and how they think. Personal contact between fellow members facilitates communication when consensus is in danger. Nonetheless, board meetings can be fraught with confrontations and tough challenges. To achieve a mutual goal, group members must be able to work together and not let personal differences create obstacles for achieving that goal — while respecting and hearing different points of view.

In the end, a board meeting is a session where those charged with being a board member gather to help shape the organization's future. When a meeting is properly orchestrated, wonderful things can happen around a board table.

MEETING, AND EXCEEDING EXPECTATIONS DISSECTS YOUR MEETINGS

Running a productive meeting seems to be a universal challenge. Who hasn't experienced a mind-numbing budget meeting, a committee meeting that accomplished nothing, a team meeting that simply rubberstamped the team leader's decisions, or a board meeting where the process clearly mattered more than the results?

Why is this, given that nearly every bookstore has an array of books on how to run meetings? It may be because many of these books focus only on parliamentary order, logistical problems, or the mechanics of meetings — all important in their own right. But isn't it the human factor that mostly creates the problems but also helps a group to conquer obstacles? The most fundamental problems tend to relate to board meetings where the presentation of informational reports clearly matters more than discussion and deliberation. After all, the boardroom is the "cradle" where the board shapes governance issues and decides on the future of its nonprofit. Balancing meaningful structure and effective communication provide a valuable basis for a board meeting that matters.

For years, BoardSource has addressed thousands of questions about boring, dysfunctional, or unproductive board meetings. Questions range from how to get members to attend meetings to how to control a domineering chair. Some ask for solutions to eliminate interminable sessions or improve minutes taking. Others ask whether the chief executive should be present at executive sessions or whether the public should be allowed to attend meetings. BoardSource has listened to the board members, chief executives, and chairs who have contacted us with their meeting issues. *Meeting, and Exceeding Expectations* (which was titled *Meet Smarter* in a previous edition) is built on the communication we have had with our customers, clients, and supporters.

WHO SHOULD READ *MEETING, AND EXCEEDING EXPECTATIONS*?

This book is designed to facilitate the work of the chief executive and the board chair, the key partners responsible for planning and orchestrating board meetings.

Its purpose is to invite board members, chairs, and chief executives to analyze their meetings and improve them. Boards with meeting problems should feel free to change old traditions. Sometimes bad meetings turn out to be expressions of other challenges the board may be facing, such as a power struggle between board members and the executive committee. Other times, poorly managed meetings turn into unnecessary stumbling blocks to achieving the board's objectives. Without a thorough understanding of the purpose of a meeting and an expectation of concrete outcomes, boards may find it difficult to change bad meeting habits. Boards should evaluate their meetings and make a commitment to turn them into productive and enjoyable events that shape the future of the organization. This book helps chief executives and chairs to determine the primary causes for their poor or boring meetings and to choose the best options to treat the problem.

And finally, this book is for the numerous board and staff members who have contacted BoardSource since 1988, educating us about the challenges they struggle with in their boardrooms. Their experiences and frustrations have been the major impetus to create this resource.

WHAT WILL YOU FIND IN *MEETING, AND EXCEEDING EXPECTATIONS*?

This book poses questions, provides answers, suggests tools, clarifies legal and ethical expectations, and shows you how to insert some fun into board meetings.

Chapter 1 examines the laws related to nonprofit board meetings. It discusses the general principles behind Sunshine Laws and outlines what the organization's bylaws should say about board meetings.

Chapter 2 focuses on thorough preparation as a key to productive board meetings. This chapter presents the how, when, and where of planning a board meeting. The chief executive and the chair may be the brains behind successful meeting planning, but it is the staff that has the often thankless task of arranging the details and logistics. Productive meeting planning takes intellectual capital as well as thoughtful organization.

A board is at its best when it communicates effectively, both during and in between meetings. But in the spirit of good communication, board members may often be flooded with documents to read: meeting minutes, agendas, and reports. Without these reporting mechanisms, however, there would be no permanent record of the board's discussions and decisions. Chapter 3 addresses the content of a variety of board documents, the value of a consent agenda, and the legal protections documentation provides the board.

Chapter 4 looks at the process of how boards structure their meetings, make decisions, and vote. You will find alternatives to using strict parliamentary order and a variety of decision-making methods.

Chapter 5 introduces the participants who must be present or who have the power to influence the outcome of a meeting. There is no meeting without board members; they must be present. The chief executive is the catalyst for the meeting and helps the board to focus on key issues. For the chair, the meeting is the forum for guiding the board into action. Numerous outsiders have a stake in successful board meetings, and it is necessary to understand who can or should be present and who should not.

Bringing a group together for a common purpose naturally is colored by the individual motivations, personalities, and characteristics of the members. A boardroom is no exception. Chapter 6 discusses some of the challenges that conflicts of interest, private agendas, and cultural differences can create during a board meeting.

Board meetings are not the only meetings where board members congregate. Board members may find themselves in committee meetings or executive sessions, at retreats, and in other special meetings. Chapter 7 discusses the particular demands and characteristics of these gatherings.

Throughout the book you will read about real life situations common to boards, such as poor chair performance, absentee board members, and conflicts of interest. Question-and-answer sidebars provide easy tools to help solve some board dilemmas or promote preventative discussion. During the past two decades, tens of thousands of board members and chief executives have contacted BoardSource with their meeting problems. We present some of them as examples in this book. Use our suggestions to help your board members become more innovative and seek new solutions to old problems.

Also included are appendices to the text with sample documents, a glossary of terms, and suggested resources for further study.

CASE STUDY
MISSING IN ACTION

Stefan, the board chair of XYZ Organization, should have called the board meeting to order 15 minutes ago, but there were not enough individuals present to make a quorum. In the past, many of the absent board members had valid reasons for not attending meetings, but they didn't always ask to be excused.

Suddenly, four more members of the board entered the room. The group now had a quorum. Stefan called the meeting to order, indicating that the board should start planning a retreat to discuss strategic planning.

One member who punctually attended each and every meeting took issue with Stefan's suggestion, however. "What," she blurted out, "is the point of going forward with a board retreat if not every member will be present? And are all board members aware of the clause in the bylaws that states, 'Absence from three board meetings within a fiscal year, without prior notification, is equivalent to resignation from the board'?"

Stefan now realized that he and the board could no longer ignore the issue of poor attendance.

Attending board meetings regularly to contribute actively in discussions and decision making is a basic board member duty. Stefan and the board can address the attendance problem by taking one or more of the following actions:

- Work with the absent board members to identify why they are missing meetings and to explore what could help them overcome the obstacles. This should be done before a member misses three meetings.

- Reduce the number of meetings to help ensure full attendance. Depending on their missions, most organizations can, with the help of consent agendas, get all their work done in bimonthly meetings and an annual retreat. Between full meetings, committees can accomplish much of the board's work. And in practice, many committees don't meet in person. They get a lot done via e-mail and phone calls, which would make participation easier and more effective for people.

- Communicate board member duties during the recruitment process. This communication should address proper "notification of absenteeism."

- Form a governance committee to oversee the development, education, and orientation of board members to their crucial duties, one of which is to attend meetings.

- Abide by the bylaws. Members must know that there are no exceptions — it is essential to fulfill their legal duty of care.

Adapted from the September/October 2007 (Volume 16, Number 5) edition of *Board Member*.

CHAPTER 1
THE LAW AND MEETINGS

Q I sit on a board of a housing development organization. Recently we adopted a confidentiality agreement that prohibits board members, including those who are residents in our development, from disclosing matters that are under consideration by the board until a vote has taken place. This is creating a tremendous amount of distrust and paranoia among the residents who are the beneficiaries of our services. Are these confidentiality agreements really common?

A Boards deal with all sorts of sensitive information affecting clients, donors, employees, and volunteers. In particular, boards are often exposed to confidential information critical to the well-being of the organization. Not only is a confidentiality policy a good business practice, it is important to the organization's credibility and reputation. Board members have legal responsibilities to fulfill, and they need to feel secure to discuss details that lead to good decisions.

A sudden change in policies may raise questions, but the policy change is a sign that the board is taking its role seriously. Board discussions should not leave the boardroom. For instance, when a board meets in executive session, typically only voting board members (and the chief executive, as appropriate) are allowed in the room. It does not mean that something fraudulent or bad is happening. It just means that details or aspects of deliberation are legally not public information and should not be shared. A policy in formation could also lead to misinformation and inappropriate lobbying of board members.

Because a board meeting is the authoritative and legitimate setting where the board makes organizational decisions, a legal framework provides support and guidance.

It also provides some comfort for founders and new board members who are struggling with their first endeavor and have no direction on how to proceed. Understanding the purpose of the laws and their relationship to good practices is necessary for all meeting participants.

Federal laws do not address board meeting processes. Since most nonprofits are organized as nonprofit corporations, they are subject to the laws of the state where they are incorporated. This book touches on several issues that state laws address — frequency of meetings, quorums, majority rule, and proxy votes, among others.

The most important aspect of legal quandaries is not just to know the laws but to understand their function. Laws do not offer the best solutions for nonprofits. Laws give only de minimis — or minimum — values for a case. For example, if a state law says that a nonprofit must have at least three members on its board, that should not be interpreted to say three members is an ideal board size. Neither does it say that a board of four or even 15 members is better. It says that with two, one, or no board members the nonprofit is functioning against the law.

RUNNING MEETINGS UNDER SUNSHINE LAWS

All states have particular regulations that apply to organizations receiving public funding: These are called sunshine laws or open meeting laws. Their purpose is to bring "sunshine" or transparency to the processes of these nonprofits and show the public how they carry out their business. Board meetings are covered by these regulations. Nonprofits that receive government funding or government contracts are usually affected by sunshine laws.

THE LAW SAYS...

Sunshine laws vary in their specificity. Some serve as general guides; others address every conceivable detail of your meeting arrangement.

- In California, meetings must be held within the boundaries of the jurisdiction of the organization.

- In Oregon, an executive session may constitute the entire meeting.

- In Wisconsin, meeting notice must be announced at least two hours before the meeting starts.

- In Utah, names and content of those commenting during the meeting must be included in the minutes.

- Virginia lists more than 20 different situations in which closed meetings may be held.

- In Colorado, if e-mail is used to discuss public business, it counts as a meeting and is therefore public information.

Sunshine laws were originally created for public bodies, specifically the government. The Sunshine Act followed the passing of the Freedom of Information Act in 1966. As taxpayers, concerned Americans want to feel comfortable that the government is using their tax dollars in a responsible manner. The same principle applies to charities that benefit from tax breaks and use tax money to advance their missions.

Some states are quite broad in their definitions of their open meeting laws; some are very detailed and meticulous. These laws may define what a meeting is, which meetings must be open to the public, how to post meeting notices, where and when a meeting may be held, which rules apply to executive sessions, how meeting minutes are shared, and so forth. The laws also state what the penalties are if organizations do not comply: Fines can be high and all decisions at the meeting may be voided. The Reporters Committee for Freedom of the Press Web site at www.rcfp.org/tapping/index.cgi is a helpful tool, providing state-by-state guidelines on sunshine laws. It is important to know your state laws and set them as the minimum requirement for your board.

Q **How do we retain control of a potentially contentious meeting? We announced budget cuts, and those affected are planning to attend the meeting and offer public comment.**

A First, make sure that you provide good explanations for your budget cuts. They may not ease the pain for those affected, but they will put the cuts in a bigger context.

Second, your board meetings are board business meetings. The board determines who is invited to attend. If you fall under the sunshine laws, then outsiders can attend your meetings. This does not mean that you should tolerate disruption or that outsiders can take charge. Your chair should clarify the rules at the beginning of the meeting, and explain that there are procedures to follow. If you allow public comments during the meeting, again, clarify the rules and invite representatives to speak at the right moment. You should expect civil behavior from everyone, no matter how contentious the issue is.

If you expect a specific outside group to attend, contact its leader or members ahead of time and discuss the above. You may want to propose another setting to hear them in more detail. And be prepared to present your big picture explanation. When things get tough, and the board has to make tough decisions, communication is the key. Don't shut yourself off. On the contrary, take a commentator's role and anticipate — as you already seem to do — what is going to happen.

Most open meeting laws provide for a venue for handling confidential issues. Each board must have the opportunity to privately discuss personnel (or patient) issues and records; consult with legal counsel about potential or pending court cases, security arrangements, business negotiations, chief executive compensation, and performance discussions; and address other confidential issues. Social gatherings of board members and educational meetings are not usually covered by sunshine laws.

The purpose of the sunshine laws is not to create an opportunity for disgruntled staff members or unhappy constituents to disrupt business proceedings. To keep meetings professional and civil, the board should clarify the kind of behavior allowed in the boardroom. For example, attendees may be allowed to make comments at the end of the meeting. Board members should pay special attention to running an effective and efficient meeting. If the board meeting is going to operate in a glass bowl, why not show the board's best side to those who are watching? Who knows, the media might also be in attendance.

WHAT SHOULD THE BYLAWS SAY ABOUT BOARD MEETINGS?

The best way for any organization to reconcile existing laws with its own needs is to study the laws; discuss openly what works best and what options provide the most equitable, ethical, or reasonable guidelines; and then clearly define the chosen approach in the bylaws. For instance, the bylaws should state whether the board follows a particular parliamentary guide or relies on reaching decisions by other methods. Bylaws serve as the internal and binding legal document for the board and are not permitted to contradict state laws. Please see Chapter 4 for additional discussion of parliamentary order.

The bylaws must provide clear guidance for how a board goes about making decisions, for example, explaining that the board uses the consensus-building method to reach agreements. The bylaws should not, however, get into the nitty-gritty aspect of process and procedure. Those should be clarified in separate guidelines, policies, and resolutions and shared with new board members in a separate policy manual or the board handbook. The bylaws should cover the issues that tend to create contentions among board members when disagreements surface. These specific areas may deal with the method of selecting board members, how to enforce term limits, or when to remove a board member. If the bylaws do not address these issues, board meetings may turn into battlegrounds or a member may later question the validity of a decision.

If the bylaws do not address state law issues dealing with meetings, normally the law ends up determining the rules. The bylaws should not contradict the law but can be stricter than the law. In addition to addressing parameters for how often the board meets and what the quorum and voting requirements are, the bylaws should clarify whether the board may meet via teleconference or rely on other technological means to bring board members together. They should clarify who can call a special meeting, whether action can be taken without a meeting, and what happens to members who miss meetings. They should not specify the dates or places of meetings, how to write minutes, or set agendas ahead of time.

REMEMBER

- Know your state laws and how they affect your board meetings.

- If you get public funding, be prepared to open your meetings to the public.

- Make sure your bylaws define your primary meeting processes — and follow them.

CASE STUDY
YOUTH MOVEMENT

Heather had volunteered for the Literacy Council since high school, giving up weekends to meet with learning-disabled young people and adults and recruiting other teens at her school as volunteers. When Jason, the board chair, asked her to join the Council's board, she was surprised. She knew nothing about board service; the youngest board member was in his 40s; and some of the board members had kids who were nearly Heather's age.

Though Jason assured Heather that the entire board was behind the invitation, the board actually was divided over whether to include young people among its members. Some felt that young board members might energize the council. Others worried that novice candidates would be poorly suited for board work.

At her first board meeting, Heather felt like a child at a grown-up dinner party. The other members seemed to speak over her instead of to her, no one asked her opinion, and when she did speak about her experiences with learning-disabled kids, she was so nervous that her voice cracked. "That's all well and good," one member said after she finished, "but let's cut the child's play and get down to business. We have to choose either adolescent or adult programs."

Humiliated, Heather called Jason after the meeting and left a message suggesting she resign. Unbeknownst to her, days earlier, two other board members had suggested the same thing. "This board does serious work. It's no place for kids," one said.

As Jason picked up the phone, he wondered if he should accept Heather's resignation. Maybe she was too young to sit on the board. He had hoped for fresh ideas. Instead, he'd started a firestorm of controversy.

The issue here is cultural diversity in its broadest definition. Racial diversity is generally understood to be an asset-building and desirable outcome for boards. But age diversity among boards — notably the inclusion of younger members — is often not similarly well received.

The Council's board needs to be educated on the issues. It might devote a significant portion of a future board meeting to educating itself about youth literacy programs. The chief executive, who is sure to be abreast of the issues and has access to relevant qualitative and quantitative data, can plan this portion of the meeting. He or she might consider inviting a young person who has benefited from the program to speak to the board. The governance committee then should help the board determine for itself that there is a need for board participation from young professionals.

By evaluating the varied skills that everyone brings to the table, the Council's board members will come to the realization that age is not a qualification but a characteristic. Although Heather may be younger than other board members, her relative maturity and years of experience volunteering with the Council make her participation invaluable.

Adapted from the April/May 2003 (Volume 12, Number 2) edition of *Board Member®*.

CHAPTER 2
PLANNING A MEETING

Q So often I leave our board meeting feeling it was a total waste of my time. What can I do about it?

A When a board member feels his time is wasted, something is seriously wrong. Determine first whether you are the only member with this opinion or whether it is a general consensus among your fellow board members. Then pose the questions below to help you determine what the actual cause might be. (Use the rest of this book to find the right remedies for the questions.)

- Do you always know ahead of time why the meeting is taking place?

- Do you always receive adequate information ahead of time to prepare yourself for the discussion or debate?

- Does your board meet too frequently?

- Are the meetings disorganized or focusing on trivial issues?

- Are the meetings organized around informational reports only with minimal discussion items?

- Is someone dominating the meeting and thereby not allowing others to share their opinions?

- Do you feel your special skills and expertise are not being utilized?

- Have you lost some of your initial interest and enthusiasm for this organization?

Don't suffer in silence or soon this board will lose you. Talk to the chair or your trusted colleagues and provide feedback to your governance committee. Offer to take the lead to see that the culprits of wasted meetings are eliminated.

The Boy Scouts say it best: Be prepared. Meetings require advance preparation to ensure that they are productive, stay on course, and receive full participation from all attendees. The most effective board meetings happen after successfully coordinated efforts of board and staff. There must be someone authorized or expected to call the meeting, compile materials, set the agenda, and handle all the logistics. And participants must do their share and their homework. Orchestration of a board meeting requires time, resources, and selfless effort.

Every chief executive knows that getting ready for a board meeting takes more than a couple of hours two weeks beforehand. In many organizations, the weeks prior to board meetings contain the most hectic hours for the chief executive. Every chair knows that getting ready for a board meeting means intensive communication with the chief executive to ensure all members come to the meeting and the focus of the meeting remains on the right issues.

WHAT IS THE PURPOSE OF THIS MEETING?

Not all meetings that bring board members together fit the same mold. There are numerous purposes for the board to convene (and beyond that, each meeting may have multiple agenda items). The purpose then determines the extent of advance preparation and expectations for the outcomes. Some meetings may only require part of the board to be present (e.g., a committee meeting).

When determining the purpose of the meeting, it is also necessary to clarify the expected outcomes. The goals for a retreat would be very different from those of an informational gathering. Tying expectations to purpose helps the participants prepare in an effective manner and helps to evaluate whether the goals and objectives were met.

Particularly for working boards with little or no staff, meetings can have a variety of objectives. Some objectives may simply be to exchange information and others to prepare for an upcoming decision or activity. Certain issues — strategic planning, capital campaigns, major acquisitions — need thorough research and discussion even before a decision can be made to launch the endeavor. At these types of meetings, it is understood ahead of time that no all-conclusive voting will take place at the end of the meeting.

Although some meetings may be called simply to share information, pure information sharing in most cases is easiest to accomplish via phone, e-mail, or in writing. Many local community boards, however, find it constructive and motivating to get together when important announcements are made or new issues surface that may have major implications for the organization or the board as a whole. The benefits of an information-sharing gathering may turn out to be a demonstration of responsiveness to community concerns or simply to get buy-in or support for an initiative.

Boards that meet only quarterly usually convene for comprehensive board meetings where deliberation leads to a final decision — or to a decision that necessitates further research before a final vote can be cast. For these boards, most of the information sharing and preparation takes place between board meetings.

Every board, without a doubt, can benefit from a retreat or board training. This provides the board an opportunity to get outside of the boardroom and reflect on its role, engage in self-assessment, discuss recruitment or fundraising challenges, explore strategic issues facing the organization, or talk about any other matters that require more time for reflection than a regular meeting can allow. For more on retreats and other meetings, see Chapter 7.

HOW OFTEN SHOULD A BOARD MEET?

It is impossible to recommend a definitive number of meetings for a board. How often a specific board needs to meet depends on many factors. Some relate to internal issues, some to external demands. Some meeting frequencies are structural; others relate to the phase in the board's lifecycle. Some are directly tied to the capacity of the board; others are determined by the load the staff takes in managing the operations. Whether the organization is local, national, or international also influences meeting frequency.

State laws, in many cases, require that nonprofits conduct one annual meeting. While it would be hard to imagine that a conscientious board could carry out all of its duties and oversight at one yearly meeting, important decisions are often made at annual meetings — electing new board members and officers, among other things. At a minimum, every board must have its annual meeting.

The most important factor determining how often the board should meet is the amount of work that needs to be accomplished. Different boards are involved in different activities. For instance, a founding board is likely to meet frequently — perhaps as often as once a month — during the start-up phase when the future of the organization is being planned and all the processes and policies are being drafted. This type of a board may also have to manage all of the logistical matters of establishing the physical working space. In addition, with no staff to share the workload, the board may have to divide operational tasks between individuals and committees or task forces to ensure that everything gets done. For a more mature board with sufficient staff to handle all operational issues, the board may meet quarterly and only focus on bigger critical issues, such as approving the budget, preparing the organization for the future, monitoring the success factors of the organization as well as ensuring that its own well-being and efficiency are always met.

A When board members show signs of burnout and indicate that their workload is unreasonable, it is time to find the culprit for this condition. Perhaps some of the following solutions would work for your board.

- Reassess the size of your board. Too small a board does not allow a wide distribution of the workload.

- If you are going through a transition period — such as the unexpected resignation of your chair or a search for a new chief executive — your capacity may be strained temporarily. Understand that this is a temporary situation. Don't let it become your standard!

- Redistribute appropriate tasks among staff and task forces. Evaluate the work done by your permanent committees and encourage them to reassess their working methods as well.

- Share tips and tools for efficient work habits.

- Test different meeting frequencies and lengths of meetings. You may be surprised how the same amount of work can be accomplished in fewer hours.

- Review your past meeting agendas. Is your board involved in board work or veering off course and focusing on operations? If so, this is the moment to fix it.

A board that is going through an internal shake-up or is trying to meet an organizational challenge may need to increase the number of meetings from its regular schedule. Perhaps the board is losing a key member, is hiring its first chief executive, or is in the middle of a strategic planning process. Flexibility and possibly additional time commitment are necessary if the full board's involvement is required. There are justified situations — loss of the chief executive, sudden financial stress, recent fraudulent activity — when the board needs to be working more closely with staff without overstepping the boundaries towards micromanagement. The full board may need to meet more frequently to brainstorm and decide together how to address and monitor these situations.

Emergencies may suddenly bring the full board together. If there is no executive committee or other processes to handle unexpected events, every board member may need to make an effort to attend and determine how to get the organization through a sudden crisis or problematic phase.

Meeting frequency is also impacted by a board member's place of residency. Regional and local boards generally meet more frequently because proximity makes it easier to convene the board, while national and international boards may find it more challenging to bring members together more than a few times a year.

It is not always easy to determine what actually requires the full board's presence or when other groups (task forces, committees, etc.) can step in to eliminate the need for gathering the full board. When setting up the yearly meeting schedule, take some time to first clarify this issue. Is the board involved in activities that cannot or should not be delegated elsewhere? Committees and task forces are there to bear a big load of board preparation work. The purpose of these subgroups is to allow the board to deal with big issues at the decision level and to not have to spend valuable meeting time digging up facts, formulating arguments, and drafting final documents. Remember also that most committee members are board members, and committee meetings and board meetings together may add up to a substantial number of meetings. Active board members face burnout if their life is filled with meetings. Respect people's private lives, and call a meeting only when necessary.

If the board meets monthly, it must be able to justify that frequency. If there is no staff, the board probably needs to be touching base in order to determine the next set of tasks and monitor progress. Boards that have competent staff support and an adequate and capable committee system may be able to justify meeting less frequently.

In order to determine whether the board should meet less frequently, consider the following questions:

- Does the board have trouble delegating? Work groups and the chief executive are there to do to the prep work. The full board should enter in the picture when the issue is presented in the board meeting.

- Is the board too operational? By stepping into the domain of the chief executive, the board spends meeting time doing staff work while disregarding its own role and purpose.

- Does the work of the board burn out its members? Sharing work is the way to spread the load and eliminate unnecessary meetings.

- Does the board structure its meetings poorly? Too-strict operating rules tend to focus more on process than on results. There is a happy medium.

- Does the board focus on short-term issues and lose the big picture? Staff is there to run the daily, weekly, and monthly matters. The board is there to address the results and monitor the progress.

- Does the board add unnecessary expenses? Every meeting costs money. Unnecessary meetings add unnecessary expenses.

- Is the staff burdened with meeting preparation? If the staff's major work load consists of getting ready for another board meeting, it is not able to find time to do its regular work.

- Does the board use other venues and communication inadequately? E-mails and phone can handle most of the pure information sharing.

Some boards may not meet often enough. It is hardly adequate for most boards to meet only once a year at the legally required annual meeting. It is highly unlikely that an accountable board is able to manage its governance responsibilities along with other duties in just a few hours. And when the board is inattentive, it may miss important yet subtle signals that something is not right, or it can miss opportunities knocking at the door. It is also very difficult to create a sense of camaraderie among board members if the board meets so infrequently.

> **Q** My board meets only once a year because members live all over the world and getting together is difficult. Sometimes, as the chief executive, I ask myself whether we need this board at all, since the organization seems to thrive without it. Am I concerned unnecessarily?

A Your board may meet the legal requirements but it probably is not adding much value to the organization. A responsible board does more than approve the budget, elect new board members and officers, and sign off on the strategic plan. It is also exists to anticipate challenges and prepare the organization for them. Your staff keeps the operations and programs going but is missing out on the input and wisdom of the collective mind of a board. Board members functioning simply as individual advisors are missing the opportunity to gain insights from each other and constructively lead the organization as a group. Investigate methods to bring the full board together at least a few times a year, such as teleconferencing, varying locations, reassessing the composition of your board, and forming regional advisory groups.

THE WHEN, WHERE, AND HOW OF PLANNING A MEETING

How often has lunch been the best part of a meeting? Perhaps the room was overwhelmingly stuffy or too cold, or the timing was complicated by work obligations or family schedules. It is only human to be affected by the "peripheries" of meeting logistics. If the organizers do not understand some basic aspects of human nature, a meeting can lose its impact.

Handling board meeting logistics is usually the job of the staff. Keeping detailed records and reminders of past groundwork can eliminate many repeated troubles. Equally, chief executives who have been present in numerous board meetings should guide the rest of the staff involved in preparations. Experience can be a powerful educator and should be used to its fullest.

Numerous logistical aspects can impact a board meeting and its outcome. The planners' main objective should be to motivate every single board member to attend the meeting, come well prepared, participate constructively, feel invigorated and energized about the work, and remember the meeting positively because of what was accomplished and because it was a pleasant and conducive place to work at that moment. Professional attitude and experienced meeting management can take you far.

WHEN SHOULD THE MEETING BE SCHEDULED?

Finding the optimal time to get every board member to come to a meeting can be a major challenge. The schedule may need to accommodate busy business people who travel often, employees who may have difficulties with leaving their work during business hours, parents who cannot leave children alone at night, young members who are in class during afternoon hours, members who rely on public transportation schedules, and so on. Also, when looking at the annual calendar, take into account major vacation periods and religious holidays.

Board members should determine the schedule together and get feedback from everyone. Some members may prefer to meet midday; others may be able to come only in the evening; some may choose weekends. Individual members may need to demonstrate a little flexibility — particularly for those who have to travel long distances. The board may want to occasionally change the meeting time to accommodate those participants who are always making compromises. If a board has an established meeting schedule, prospective members should be told before they accept the nomination.

HOW LONG SHOULD THE MEETING LAST?

The agenda determines the length of the meeting. Naturally, the goal is to maximize the use of time. There needs to be a balance between getting business done and allowing sufficient time for personal interaction. Here are some questions that could help the board determine the appropriate length for meetings.

- **How often does the board meet?**

  If it is monthly, under normal circumstances business could take an hour or so. If it is only a few times a year, the meeting could last a full day or more.

- **What is the purpose of the meeting?**

  Regularly scheduled board meetings may follow an expected pattern as outlined in the annual meeting agenda, but the length for special or emergency sessions is defined by the urgency and importance of the issue. Retreats can stretch out over a weekend.

- **How skilled is the board chair in conducting a meeting?**

  Keeping the discussion focused and following the agenda are some of the qualities of an able chair. A good facilitator is able to respect the predetermined length of the meeting.

- **Is the agenda appropriate?**

  Board meetings are for board business. Adopting a consent agenda, a compilation of items that the board approves with one vote, allows the board to concentrate on timely and big picture issues.

- **Is staff getting appropriate materials to board members well before the meeting?**

  A meeting can be shortened when board members have done their homework and arrive well prepared and familiar with the agenda items and support materials.

The board chair has the major responsibility of getting everyone appropriately engaged. Without apt participation, it can be difficult to control the length of the meeting. The meeting can turn out to be a monologue presented by the chair or some other participant (lack of member engagement), a lengthy session with endless comments (lack of control), or there can be a balanced process where sharing of ideas leads to productive conclusions.

WHERE SHOULD THE BOARD MEET?

For a national or an international organization, the location of the board meeting can have major financial implications — both for individual members and for the organization itself. If board members travel by plane or drive for hours, they may find it difficult to justify going a long distance for just a two-hour meeting. If time and location dictate, some members might like to tie in other business or pleasure travel with the board meeting schedule. Arranging a meeting in a major city or vacation resort can become an added incentive to attending. If meetings are always in the same location, some board members may have a bigger burden to bear — money, time, and effort — while local members are always in a more advantaged position. If meetings take place outside the office, factor in the operational costs for travel and hotels for senior staff in attendance with the expense of a suitable meeting place.

For a local organization, choosing a meeting venue is also a key issue. Should it happen at the office? Are there suitable conference facilities nearby? If the organization's office has a large enough conference or meeting room, that can be an excellent solution. Holding meetings in the office can provide the opportunity for staff to meet the board members. Making board members visible to staff demystifies the board — even if board work mostly happens behind a closed door. Arranging for the staff to join the board for lunch or dinner provides an opportunity for board-staff interaction.

If the office cannot accommodate a full board meeting, research other options in the area. Most areas have conference facilities suitable for small and large groups and for every budget. A board member may even be able to offer his or her business site for a meeting, free of charge. Small grassroots boards may choose to meet at the home of a board member when the cost of renting a meeting space cannot be justified — even if this is not the ideal option. Smaller boards often embrace camaraderie and cooperation, but to keep the business aspect of the meetings from being overcome by the social aspect, it is important that the meeting space provide a congenial but private setting for serious discussion.

TIP

NEW LOCATIONS FOR BOARD MEETINGS

Consider looking beyond the traditional boardroom setting for regular board meetings or even for a board retreat. Imagine having the next meeting

- at a hospital, school, museum, university campus, or library — whatever is most appropriate for the mission of the organization

- at a setting chosen by a board member who hosts the occasion

- on a cruise ship, where board members' families may come along (at their own expense, of course)

- in a bus touring the surroundings of the community

- during a picnic, after a bird-watching trip, at the end of a hiking outing — whatever fits the personalities or hobbies of the board members and the activities of the organization

- at the facilities of a major funder

As with timing, it is possible to impact attendance by changing the location every so often. If the board members live within driving distance, choose a different town for different meetings. Let board members host the meetings or provide feedback on possible locations within their community. If the meeting location changes on a regular basis, make sure that the board has plenty of advance notice about the new location along with clear driving directions.

HOW SHOULD THE ROOM BE SET UP?

Whether the issue is who sits where or the temperature of the room, details can determine the attentiveness of board members during a meeting. Having predetermined seating arrangements may be important. Where does the chief executive sit? Under most circumstances, the chief executive sits next to the board chair. This sends a signal that the chief executive position is crucial — even if he or she is not a voting member of the board. This seating arrangement indicates that there is an established partnership between the chair and the chief executive and it helps facilitate communication between the two. This arrangement does not necessarily apply during retreats or at some committee meetings where the board chair and the chief executive are also present.

The board may choose to have assigned seating arrangements for all participants. If so, change the order regularly. This will encourage members to communicate directly with peers who may not always share their opinions. These configurations can change the dynamics of communication channels. If seats are not assigned, simply invite board members to sit next to someone with whom they do not usually interact or next to someone whom they don't know very well. Developing personal connections is a way to encourage interaction among colleagues.

Q During our board meetings, the same people always sit next to each other and this seems to lead to cliques and divisiveness. How can we change this?

A In a gathering people tend to sit next to friends or others with whom they are comfortable. By addressing this tendency, you might succeed in getting your board members to know each other better and even to shed some preconceived ideas they might have about each other. Here are some suggestions to change seating arrangements either intentionally or haphazardly.

- Assign seats before the meeting with place cards and change the order regularly.

- Ask board members to sit next to the colleague whom they know the least well.

- As they enter, let board members draw a number and then sit in numerical order.

- Seat everyone in alphabetical order.

Attendees with no actual role in the meeting should sit on the periphery of the boardroom and not mix with board members. A staff member or guest invited to make a presentation or participate in an important discussion should be treated with respect. Welcome participating staff to sit around the boardroom table. Seat guest speakers next to the board chair. In many cases, the guests will stay for only a portion of the meeting, but it is essential for them to understand that their role is important and appreciated during the time they are present.

Seating arrangements can influence the outcome of a meeting. Different table formations may affect the ease with which members communicate with each other. At a round table everyone is on equal footing, though some say a round table hinders decision making as the chair of the meeting does not "appear" to be in a position of authority, such as at the head of the table. A classroom-style seating arrangement is counterproductive, even for larger groups as it forces board members to talk to the back of their peers and never have eye contact with them. Long narrow tables seat some participants far from the chair and encourage side discussions across the table. Face-to-face seating allows for open discussion and eye contact but it can also feed fire to deliberation as "opponents" choose different sides to the table and read each other's eyes. There may not be a choice in the shape of the table, but a broad, rectangular table tends to work well.

Physical comfort is another aspect that affects the participants. Before the meeting, test the temperature of the meeting room. Find out how to change it if it gets too hot or too cold. Remember that dim lights make people sleepy. There may not be much choice about the chairs on which attendees will sit, but test them anyway. If the organization is in the process of equipping its office conference room, do not make the mistake of choosing chairs simply for their low cost or elegance. Board members will be sitting on those chairs in that room for hours at a time, so make sure that this side of meeting planning — overall comfort — makes attending meetings a less taxing experience.

FEEDING THE BOARD

Food represents a social aspect of a board meeting. If a meal is served in the middle of a meeting, that is a time when business is secondary and more relaxed conversation can take place. Mealtime can be a time to build relationships and trust among board members. It is easier to relate to peers when they let their guard down, exchange personal news, and talk without the constant guidance or reference from the board chair. Naturally, the minutes don't reflect these casual chats.

It is a good idea to provide some refreshments during a meeting. Provide light breakfast items if the meeting starts early in the morning and serve coffee, water, and soft drinks during breaks. Serving lunch is a given if a meeting goes through noontime. Some boards meet over dinner after working hours. Whenever food is served, it is important to separate business from eating. It can be difficult to get the board's full attention on business if the participants are worrying about their salad dressing, or if the restaurant is noisy. If wine is offered at the meeting, wait to serve it until the end of the business — and always provide water or a soft drink alternative. These little measures help keep boredom and fatigue at bay.

TIP
SOCIALIZING

Consider hosting a dinner the night before the board meeting takes place. This is a perfect time for socializing, inviting senior staff into the more intimate board circle, and setting the tone for the next day.

HOW MUCH WILL IT COST?

Board meetings cost money — there is no way around it. Make sure that the annual governance budget includes a "meetings" item. Keep track of the current or previous year's receipts and it will be easier to budget expenses for the following year.

Larger boards naturally mean larger expenses. The direct items to factor into the budget include the cost of a meeting room, catering, and photocopying and postage for mailing board books if they are not sent electronically.

If the board does have a travel reimbursement policy, as discussed below, all compensation expenses should be included as a line item in the meetings budget. Staff may spend a significant amount of time preparing for the meetings, so staff time should be anticipated and accounted for in time sheets.

◗━◆ TIP
COSTLY MEETINGS

Staff members want to keep board members happy and often go out of their way to ensure a high-quality meeting setting. As board members are not paying the bill out of their own pockets, they happily come to a "comfortable" meeting that resembles what they are used to in their own business meetings. To keep meeting expenses from getting out of line, add a line to your next meeting assessment: "Give three suggestions on how to cut our meeting costs without sacrificing quality." With this approach, you engage your board members in brainstorming ways they can positively affect the bottom line.

The budget may also need to include any additional operating costs for committee meetings. Because the cost of meetings comes from the organizational budget, carefully calculate where the line is between appropriate and adequate. Some board members may be used to expensive restaurants and fancy accommodations in their private or business lives. This does not mean that the board needs to follow the example and cater to the members' personal preferences. Each organization must determine for itself what standards it considers appropriate. For instance, the board of a community soup kitchen would not bring in a famed caterer to feed its board members.

Q **What are our options for meeting expense reimbursement for board members?**

A Before adopting a reimbursement policy, your board needs to look at the issue from all angles. Individual board members and the organization's budget are directly affected by this policy.

The cost of attending board meetings should not create undue financial burden for any board member. Regional and national boards sometimes have a special challenge in this regard. The cost of coming to meetings may prevent some valuable candidates from joining your board. At the same time, transferring the financial burden to your organization is not necessarily the best or easiest solution. These expenses add up quickly, and they come out of the organization's budget.

Remember also: No matter how effective the board is, funders would much rather put their money behind an organization's programmatic needs than its board members' travel expenses.

Here are possible options when your board decides to adopt a meeting attendance reimbursement policy.

Option 1: Do not reimburse. Your board members accept the personal responsibility to absorb all the costs. If your board decides to take this route, the policy must be communicated to prospective board members. Board member candidates must feel comfortable about personally assuming the future expenses associated with board meeting attendance. Another suggestion: Ask board members to turn these expenses into tax-deductible contributions to the organization to count against meeting expenses.

Option 2: Reimburse upon request. Allow individual board members to determine whether they need reimbursement or are willing and able to pay all or part of their own expenses. This option accommodates those members for whom service would otherwise be impossible.

Option 3: Reimburse expenses. Set acceptable caps and standards to control the overall cost. Include the expense cost item in your budget.

If your board decides to reimburse some expenses, it should explain the details in a separate policy.

- Stipulate a ceiling per board member per meeting, determine a manageable per diem, or clarify the fine points of what is acceptable and what is not. These points may cover mileage reimbursement rates, a list of acceptable hotels or dollar limits for hotel stays, or whether board members are expected to fly coach.

- Determine a differentiation between travel to committee meetings and board meetings. Some local boards with members in the lowest income bracket reimburse lost wages for the time spent in a board meeting or contribute to babysitter fees for single parents of small children.

- Paying spouses' expenses should be justified judiciously. Under most circumstances it is not appropriate. This reimbursement may turn into a compensation issue that must be reported in the Form 990.

MEETINGS WITHOUT A BOARDROOM

Sometimes it is impossible for a board member to be physically present at a board meeting, whether due to geography, an unavoidable business conflict, or personal matters. How is a board to accommodate a member who wants to be part of the meeting but is not able to be present physically? What options are there to organize a meeting when everyone is not able to sit around the same table?

Cost cutting also can be a motivation for looking into new ways to run meetings without losing effectiveness and missing opportunities for board members to get to know their peers.

First, check your state laws. Laws change slowly and do not simulate the speed-of-light technological evolution of our society. Electronic communication is a way of life today, no longer a specialty of the younger generation. Boards are becoming more computer savvy and learning to take advantage of electronic opportunities. However, meeting and voting via cyberspace are still highly controversial — and rightly so — and must be considered with care. Some state statutes specifically recognize the legitimacy of teleconference or videoconference attendance. If your laws do not forbid these types of meetings, embrace them as excellent methods to bring flexibility to your meeting planning and to board communication in general. As a rule, if it is possible to establish a quorum, allow everyone to express opinions separately, keep track of the flow of the meeting and voting results, and later produce accurate minutes; these formats can provide an absent board member with an opportunity to fulfill his or her expectations as a responsible member of the board.

Teleconferencing and videoconferencing can bring the board together quickly in an emergency, and they save costs by cutting down long-distance travel and staff involvement. They are also truly helpful for keeping committees and task forces in touch between regular meetings. It is not always necessary for everyone to sit in the same room to get business done. However, they should not replace traditonal face-to-face meetings on a regular basis.

TELECONFERENCING

Board teleconferencing is no different from other business conference calls. Participants are connected through a conference call bridge that has the capacity to accomodate multiple users simultaneously. Following common sense helps make these meetings work.

- Be mindful of different time zones. Choose a convenient hour for everyone to be a part of the meeting. If you have international board members, it is quite clear that some people need to be more flexible than others.

- Pay special attention to involving all board members in the conversation. It is easier to take an observant role when invisible. Address quiet members directly. Call them by their names. Ask for their opinions.

- Take a roll call to establish a quorum. Start the meeting by asking everyone to state their name. Even phone meetings need a quorum.

- Ask every speaker to first identify herself before making a comment. Phone voices are not always easily recognizable. This is also the only way the minutes taker can tie a comment or a motion to the right individual.

- Don't allow people to speak at the same time. If every person first identifies him or herself, it is a bit more difficult to interrupt. Naturally the chair needs to control a verbose member.

- Ask members to call from a quiet location and speak clearly. Background noises tend to be magnified when you are on a speaker phone.

- Don't use teleconferencing for major planning meetings or for sorting out a conflict. Lengthy, demanding discussions benefit from open, face-to-face communication and may require breaks or small-group brainstorming.

- Follow up with minutes. Teleconferencing is just another form of a meeting. Proper minute-keeping is necessary.

VIDEOCONFERENCING

The advantage of videoconferencing is to allow participants to see and hear each other as the meeting proceeds. This happens by integrating video, audio, and peripherals to interact via some type of telecommunication lines. Today, synchronization of images and sounds is much improved from the early quivering pictures and belated sound transmission. The following guidelines help boards consider this option:

- Have a contingency plan in case contact is lost or interrupted. Make sure everyone has received materials ahead of time in case you need revert to teleconferencing or change locations.

- Test the system and tech sites ahead of time to avoid the pitfalls of Murphy's Law. This also helps those uninitiated to feel more comfortable in front of the camera.

- Try to find convenient contact sites for members or organize regional contact points. Your expenses will increase if you have to arrange for needed equipment for some board members.

- Include the cost in the budget but realize that you save on other expenses.

- Investigate numerous available software options allowing telephone calls to be transmitted via the Internet. They can be a cost-saving method for board members if you rely on videoconferencing as a frequent method of communication.

- Remind board members of your normal meeting protocol. Even if everyone is not sitting around the same table, you are still conducting a business meeting.

Board meeting logistics should not end up making meetings cumbersome, unnecessarily challenging, turning promising candidates away, or inhibiting members' productivity and creativity. While there is an expectation that board members place the needs of the organization above their own priorities, and therefore express understanding and show flexibility in the meeting arrangements, boards should work on a culture that understands, respects, and discusses specific individual needs board members might have. A diverse board is bound to encounter specific ethnic sensitivities and preferences. These issues are discussed in more detail in Chapter 4.

REMEMBER

- Well prepared is half done! Your objective is to create a conducive setting for a productive business meeting.

- Meet only as often as necessary to keep the board engaged and get the work done.

- Organize a meeting that encourages attendance and facilitates creativity. Pay attention to locale, timing, and the comfort of the overall setting.

- Investigate how to cut costs without cutting the incentives to bring the full board together.

CASE STUDY
BE PREPARED

Prior to every board meeting, the staff of ABC Organization faithfully pulled together pertinent reports to send to all board members at least a week before the meeting. This allowed board members to come to the meetings prepared with questions and insights. Unfortunately, not all members read the reports — such as Peter! More often than not, he wasted the board's valuable time by asking time-consuming questions about items that were clearly explained in the reports. "He talks just to prove that he is contributing," whispered one disgruntled member to another at a recent meeting. "If he would read the documents beforehand, like the rest of us do, we could use our time to actually discuss the issues and make decisions."

Having to bring someone up to date in meetings that were specifically designated for discussion and consensus based on previously provided information slows down the board and may prevent the necessary decision making from taking place as planned. When poor preparedness happens, the board chair and board can take one or more of the following actions:

- Lead a discussion with the full board about meeting preparedness and each member's obligation to refrain from commenting or giving advice in a discussion when he does not have the full information to do so. Board members can agree that preparedness will be part of the team process so it is expected each time. If it is stated as part of a meeting's standard operating procedure, the board chair is responsible for managing the process.

- Meet with Peter after the meeting to discuss his behavior and how it is affecting the group process. Ask him what advance information he might find helpful. Is he receiving too much? Not enough? What format is best in order to digest it appropriately?

- Additionally, ask the above questions annually of the entire board as a subject for ongoing board development. Not only will it surface any concerns or areas for improvement so that the process can be revised on a regular basis, but it will cultivate an aspect of organizational culture that meeting attendees will come fully prepared as an indication of respect for everyone else's time.

Adapted from *Taming the Troublesome Board Member* by Katha Kissman, BoardSource, 2006.

CHAPTER 3

MEETING DOCUMENTATION AND BOARD COMMUNICATIONS

Q As the chief executive of our small organization, I have just scheduled a meeting with my chair to plan all the issues we must remember to include in our agendas during the coming year. Can you help me brainstorm what those issues might be?

A An excellent idea! Naturally, you can't foresee all the issues that your board may need to address during the year, but with some planning you will ensure that your board does not neglect its standard duties. Find a spot for the following:

- Approve the budget for the coming year.

- Visit the budget midyear to see if any adjustments are necessary.

- Schedule a session with your auditor to review the audit.

- Elect new officers and/or board members if seats open during the year.

- Review your Form 990 before it gets filed.

- Discuss your chief executive's annual performance review.

- Schedule an annual retreat for the board.

- Distribute new conflict-of-interest disclosure forms to all board members.

- Discuss whether this is the year for review of bylaws, policies, or board self-assessment.

- Include board development moments.

- Bring in experts to address community concerns, national trends, or legal issues that might affect your organization.

Communication between board members happens on a continuum, and information exchange is a constant activity during and in between meetings. Naturally, this can be facilitated by accurate and comprehensive documents as well as a clear understanding of the boundaries between official and private communication dealing with board and organizational matters.

Board documents provide a permanent record of the board's activities, discussions, and decisions and, if properly kept, can provide the board with some legal protection. In addition to the standard board documents (meeting agendas, board minutes, board books, and meeting reports), this chapter discusses the advantages of using consent agendas and how to benefit from electronic communication between board meetings.

AGENDA AS YOUR ROAD MAP

Regardless of the purpose of the meeting, you need an agenda. The agenda is the road map — the reminder for the chair to keep the meeting moving forward and the guide for the participants to know what to expect next. (Please see agenda samples in Appendix I.) Reviewing the agenda prior to a meeting helps board members prepare mentally for upcoming discussions. Pay attention to the following issues.

Schedule. To maximize participation of all members of the board in all meetings, set the meeting schedule at least a year ahead of time. This may sound daunting, but certain issues come up every spring or fall (such as approving the annual budget or board elections) so some agenda items can be determined far in advance.

TIP
KEEPING MISSION IN FOCUS

Some boards print the mission statement on the meeting agenda, meeting minutes, and the nonprofit's letterhead. It may be printed on a poster on the wall of the boardroom. The board can also include "mission moments" in the meeting — short testimonials that demonstrate the connection between the organization and constituents in order to draw the link between the programs and their outcomes. Read a letter from a happy customer!

Focus. The organization's strategic plan or framework is a key reference to be reflected in the agenda. An organization should not go through the time and trouble of a strategic planning process and then ignore the results. Thorough planning has already identified the key topics that the board must include on its radar screen. The agenda should fit into the overall scheme that the board must follow. The board should be on top of the relevant issues and should not spend valuable meeting time discussing matters that are better handled via e-mail, phone calls, or committee deliberations.

Boards that think strategically are constantly ahead of the game and their meeting agendas will reflect this attitude. While still giving proper attention to the board's oversight responsibilities, these boards save a major part of the meeting for issue discussions that are timely and geared toward the next phase where the organization wants to be. If the organization is in the middle of a controversy or a struggle, the board looks at options for getting it back on track to meet the challenges that are still in the pipeline.

A board meeting agenda must be focused on the future. It should not dwell on the past and rehash what has already happened. A fundamental mistake in drafting agendas is to dedicate 80 percent of the meeting time to committee reports. The board is responsible for paving the future for the organization and it can only do so if it focuses on issues that are either waiting to happen or that it wants to happen. These issues affect the sustainability of the organization and should be anticipated by the board in a purposeful manner.

Q We want to include a short "governance moment" (a time during a meeting that focuses the board on a specific governance issue) on a timely or controversial topic or a tricky issue. What are some ideas for these discussions?

A It is an excellent idea to incorporate dedicated time into every meeting to focus your board members on issues, questions, or processes that are not yet well defined. These discussions can lead to a decision or indicate the need for further study. Governance moments can provide an invigorating break during the meeting. Here are some suggested topics.

- What criteria should we use to include or exclude our customers or clients as board members?

- Should we use peer review as a tool to re-elect our officers?

- What do we think about sabbaticals for our chief executive?

- What should our policy be on accepting stocks as a contribution? Should we sell or keep them?

- How could we deliberate more effectively?

Drafting the agenda. In most organizations the chair and the chief executive share the effort. In a discussion between the two, the chair ensures that topics included are appropriate for the board and that all relevant issues are incorporated. The chief executive adds topics that the board would not otherwise know, such as the organization's operational challenges and successes since the last meeting, and possible future issues the board should be prepared to tackle. Together the two leaders can prioritize the issues while ensuring that the agenda is not too staff-driven or operational but still includes the chief executive's internal perspective. It also is helpful to highlight the items in the agenda requiring board voting, perhaps providing a list of main discussion points.

Board members may sometimes request that an item be added to the agenda. The board chair reviews those requests and determines whether they require discussion by the full board or whether the issue can be handled directly with the board member or referred to a committee. It is possible also that a constituent, client, or a customer may want the board to address an issue at the next meeting. Once again, the chair is in the best position to respond. He may determine that the request is a management matter and refer the individual to the chief executive. If the issue potentially has an organization wide impact, it may be appropriate for the full board to be briefed about it and determine a course of action.

Q Our chair has refused to place an item on the agenda that two board members have requested for discussion. Does he have the right to do that? He did the same thing when a member of the community had an issue she wanted the board to address.

A The chair and the chief executive most likely have discussed this and concluded that the issue should be handled some other way. The same probably was the case with the community member matter. Board meetings are not always the most appropriate or even efficient venues for all concerns. Some cases are clear management cases, and the chief executive should put them on her calendar. Others may be best handled on a one-on-one basis or may need additional preparation or information before they come to the board. In any case, it is important that each request gets a prompt and appropriate explanation on how the issue will be dealt with and by whom.

Logistics. A board meeting agenda must convey the basic logistics for the coming meeting: where and when the meeting takes place. The agenda should clarify the type of meeting it is (board meeting, board retreat, etc.) and identify the general business: the call to order, approval of last minutes, and the adjournment. An agenda should also list the main items needing attention. As a helpful guide, it may indicate the time allotted for each item and whether the item is there for discussion, information, or action. Consider including the most important business at the beginning of the agenda to ensure that the board does not run out of time or miss those board members who may occasionally need to leave meetings early in order to catch a plane or relieve a babysitter.

One of the crucial functions of a board is to monitor and evaluate an organization's advancement in fulfilling its mission and, more specifically, in meeting previously set goals. The staff facilitates this process by providing accurate, timely, and relevant reports for the board's inspection. This cannot be accomplished simply by filling board members' mailboxes with excessive and overly detailed data. One approach staff can rely on is dashboard reporting, which makes it possible to present succinct, easily readable performance indicators that allow the board to view organizational status at a glance.

Dashboard Reporting

A crucial function of a board is to monitor and evaluate its organization's advancement in fulfilling its mission and, more specifically, in meeting previously set goals. One of the most helpful tools to that effect is a dashboard report. Usually this report, which is attached to the agenda, is a one- to two-page document with graphs, charts, tables or columns — and limited text. The document presents visual information consistent with and compared to previous data so the board can effortlessly spot changes or trends in performance. All the necessary information is in one place, not scattered in separate documents. The charts can be color-coded with dots or arrows to allow the board to immediately see when the results are on target, exceed expectations, or are lagging behind.

There is no single set of right things to measure for every organization; each board must choose what's best in regard to its current circumstances. After evaluating the overall performance and lifecycle of the organization, it is easier to determine which specific undertakings need the board's attention and what criteria — benchmarking, growth, risk management, achieving strategic goals — the board should use in determining its approach. The board naturally needs to monitor the finances of the organization, but plenty of other issues may prove just as important. Specific indicators that the board may want to monitor include the following:

- Finances: revenue and expenses, cash flow, budget projections, contributions

- Programs: client and customer participation, satisfaction levels, client flow from program to program, graduation/program completion rates

- Quality control: number of mistakes, accidents, complaints

- Human resources: turnover rate, growth of staff, compensation comparisons

Dashboard reports enable the board to do the following tasks more easily:

- Support planning — Performance indicators allow the board to see seasonal variations and patterns in activities, detect trends, and become sensitive to demographic changes.

- Identify performance drivers — Carefully chosen data link efforts to results (inputs to outputs) and align activities with each other (funding, sales, marketing) to better reach the common goals.

- Prioritize information — When the staff guides the board's focus to a few key strategic areas at a time, it avoids diffusing board members' attention, delivering too much information, and sharing unnecessary or inappropriate information.

- Identify problems early — By following the evolution of activities in a graph format and comparing it to previous data, it is easier for board members to detect shifts or see a sudden change in the results.

- Increase efficiency — Because the staff has already created a process for capturing data and presenting them in a standard, consistent format, there is no reinventing the wheel when a board meeting approaches.

At the same time it is good to remember that dashboards do not stand alone. They never replace traditional communication and information sharing with the board. Other documents present the background support for the numbers and figures and cover issues that are not addressed in the dashboard report. A board member must always understand the context within which data are shared. For example, the fundraising results this year seem disappointing — not because the annual campaign was unsuccessful, but because the results are being compared to last year when a major donor unexpectedly gave much more than the typical amount. Numbers and charts are not meant to convey all types of information. A chart cannot explain the reason behind high staff turnover or what actually brings people back to renew their subscriptions. Qualitative data do not translate well into graphics, and the appropriate stories need to be told along with and in addition to the data.

From time to time it is necessary to determine whether the right indicators are capturing the board's attention. Over time, the reports may need to change focus or the board may want to experiment with different levels of detail, identify alternative indicators, or discover new approaches to digesting the data.

CONSENT AGENDAS: HOW DO THEY HELP?

Smart boards realize that time truly is a scarce commodity and they make an effort to spend every minute of their meeting strategically and purposefully. When the full board is able to get together only a few times during the year, it is important to make that time count. This is where the consent agenda can help.

The primary benefit of adopting a consent agenda is to focus the board's attention on governance matters and liberate meetings from administrative and operational overload. If the board spends its time on passively listening to reports rather than engaging all the members in active discussion and debate, the result is inadequate governance. When the board has time to be proactive, it has a better chance to prepare the organization for the future.

A consent agenda appears as one section or one subject in the actual meeting agenda. Usually, it is placed at the very beginning of the agenda to let the board subsequently continue on with other issues that need attention.

Consent agendas allow the board to group standard, regular, and routine items under one heading and pass that "package" with one vote. The feature common to these items is that none of them should require any discussion. When the chair brings the consent agenda to a vote, if one board member has a question concerning an item included in the consent agenda, that item is pulled and handled separately. This last issue can be a challenge for boards that are not comfortable and familiar with the process. But with practice, education, and patience, a board will soon learn to appreciate consent agendas and the impact they have on the way meetings are run.

A standard consent agenda could include

- committee and chief executive reports
- approval of the minutes from the last meeting
- any routine documents that simply need to get recorded in the minutes
- other items that have previously gone through thorough deliberation and simply need the final seal of approval by the board

The board needs to be familiar and comfortable with each item it votes on in the consent agenda. This level of familiarity is possible to achieve when the documents and reports have been distributed to every board member well in advance of the meeting as part of the overall board book. The time for the board to ask questions about items on the consent agenda is in the days and weeks before the meeting. By using e-mail or a phone call to clarify a point or suggest a correction in the minutes, the person responsible for the agenda should then make the necessary changes and share the corrected version with all board members before the meeting. The board meeting is not the ideal place to handle these operational issues — that would defeat the purpose of a consent agenda.

Everyone Wins!

Adopting a consent agenda positively affects every meeting participant.

Chair: You may need to prepare more vigorously to run the meetings. Now that more time is available for deliberation, you may need to hone your facilitation techniques to ensure all active issues and every member get proper attention.

Chief executive: This is your chance to use the collective wisdom of your board members! With time for discussion, you have a chance to preface big, new issues and benefit from immediate feedback.

Board members: No passive meetings possible: Time spent listening to reports is over. And by familiarizing yourself ahead of time with the background materials for the consent agenda, you can eliminate fears of important issues passing unnoticed.

By using consent agendas, a board can save critical time for discussion of issues that need attention. Removing committee reports from the main agenda may first make committee chairs feel as if their work is not appreciated. Including the report in the consent agenda does not mean a committee's work on a crucial issue should be ignored and tabled. On the contrary, a committee's recommendation or analysis may be the focal point of the board's next discussion. Once the committee's report has been recorded, the board can move forward on the issue. It makes sense to read that report prior to the meeting rather than have it take up precious meeting time. At the same time, it is possible for a committee to meet and have nothing extremely important or pressing to share with the board. In that case, no report is necessary.

Another advantage to the consent agenda is the elimination of inactive participation. Meetings can become boring when members are required to sit still and listen to reports. Committee reports rarely make the boardroom burst into laughter because of their special humor or captivating case studies. Board members need to be stimulated and that stimulation comes from participation in an engaging debate or discussion.

PREPARING BOARD BOOKS

To ensure board members come to a meeting well prepared and ready to participate, board books should reach members at least a week before the meeting. The board book is the main tool to prepare members of the board for fruitful discussion. Information included in the book should contain all of the necessary materials and documents that address issues listed in the agenda, with the agenda itself being the main document included. (Please see a sample in Appendix II.)

In most organizations the staff is responsible, as well as best equipped, to compile the books. The chief executive is the key person to keep the board informed of relevant issues. He or she has already developed the agenda with the chair and is tuned to the details of the next meeting. The staff has the resources and the files that feed into board education and information. It is involved in industry issues that the board needs to understand along with other matters that closely relate to the organization. The staff serves as the support mechanism for board operations and ensures that every board member has what is needed to come prepared to the meeting. It is the job of the chair and the chief executive to review the board book information and ensure that the board isn't bogged down with administrative information but rather is focused on its governance and oversight responsibilities.

We live in a fast-paced, environmentally conscious world while trying to avoid unnecessary expenses. Sharing board books electronically makes sense. This distribution channel cuts costs since postage and copying are eliminated, saves staff time as collating books is no longer necessary, and provides a last-minute opportunity to update information or add a needed document. Materials posted on a member-secure intranet or Web page can be archived and easy to access after the meeting. Experience has shown, however, that board members are likely to print materials and may even ask to have them available at the meeting. Projecting the documents on a screen during the meeting may gradually wean board members from the habit of printing materials.

BOARD MEETING MINUTES
WHY KEEP MINUTES?

Minutes form a permanent record of a board meeting. They provide practical information about when the meeting took place, who was present, and what actually happened in the boardroom. They serve as the memory of the meeting. Minutes are a legal document approved by the board and can be used as support documents in the courtroom — the single most powerful message of the legal authority of minutes.

WHAT SHOULD BE INCLUDED IN THE MINUTES?

While content can vary based on each individual organization, the basic elements of good minutes include

- name of organization

- date and time of meeting

- board members in attendance, excused, and absent

- existence of a quorum

- action steps: motions made and by whom, brief account of any debate, voting results, names of abstainers and dissenters

- reports and documents introduced

- future action steps

- time meeting ended

- signature of secretary and chair

Imagine a situation where meeting minutes are not kept. Sometime later, one of the board members questions the direction another member is taking while referring to a previous decision. Both board members have a different but firm view of what the board decided. Because there is no record, they cannot reconcile and verify the facts. In another case, a board member, during a legal case based on duty of care, wants to prove to his lawyer that he actively opposed an initiative during several meetings. Because no minutes exist, he is not able to do so. In other situations it may become necessary to determine exactly when a policy was amended and approved. If minutes are not kept, this information is not obtainable.

The above examples are just a few of the possible situations where clear meeting minutes could have saved the face of a board member, eliminated unnecessary confusion and time loss, and comforted (or brought a cold sweat to the brow of) a board member who was implicated in a lawsuit. Minutes are one of the best protective mechanisms for board members. If a board keeps haphazard minutes, this document does not help when help is needed. A solid way to keep track of board decisions is to have minutes that avoid unnecessary and onerous comments and that indicate which board member approved an action, was against an action, or was absent from the meeting. To protect themselves, every board member should read the document with care before approving it.

Verification of the meeting minutes and their thoroughness should be a concern for every board member before anyone needs to rely on them for help in the future.

Is There a "Best" Way to Take and Keep Minutes?

Two things are necessary for good and accurate record keeping: (1) a competent person to take the minutes and (2) a format that delivers readable and understandable information. Today a staff member often replaces the board secretary in keeping the minutes. This person could be the executive assistant or a designated board liaison that enables the board secretary and the chief executive to participate fully in the meeting without having to focus on recording the session.

If a board needs to handle confidential issues, it should call an executive session. Any confidential notes or documents that result should not be attached to the board meeting minutes and therefore — depending on the case — remain protected under open meeting laws and during a possible court hearing.

After the contents of the minutes have been clarified (please see the previous page for a list of items and sample format in Appendix III), it is easier to decide on the format. A suitable format reflects the culture of the board and presents the facts in a concise and easily referenced manner. While deciding on a format, keep in mind that this document — despite its name — is not a story of every minute that was spent in the meeting; it is not a verbatim account. Members should not have to plow through pages and pages of who said what to whom and when. The minutes focus on decisions made and actions taken. Direct quotes during debate are not usually desirable, as they could hinder honest and candid dialogue. Summaries of discussions should be objectively reported.

A board member's vote is also reflected in the minutes. If a board member is shy about asking questions when he or she does not understand a point and votes "with the flow," that uninformed and unsure vote gets recorded whether it truly reflects the board member's opinion or not. An understanding that the minutes record each member's decision regarding an issue should force members to pay attention to the influence and strength of their votes and the document itself. Bashfulness is not an excuse in the boardroom: If a member doesn't understand something, he or she should ask a question and vote only when comfortable with the decision.

All minutes ultimately must be approved by the board. The following tips can be helpful.

- Circulate and review the minutes between meetings. A person responsible for the minutes should ensure that a copy of the draft gets to each board member and the chief executive for review and possible comments. To avoid numerous back-and-forths, a simple format and agreement on how much detail is to be included is necessary.

- E-mail minutes to board members for the simplest and quickest way to get feedback and to redistribute the document when changes are recommended.

- Include the final version in the consent agenda to avoid any additional discussion on minutes in the boardroom.

- Include a "minutes discussion" on the main agenda if it seems that getting minutes approved becomes too laborious. Have the full board decide on a mutually acceptable solution for the process and overall contents for the minutes.

Use a "minutes book" to keep all the consecutive minutes well organized as helpful reference documents. The same applies to all board resolutions. This book may be a binder that contains the record of all minutes — usually kept in the organiztion's office — or an electronic file made accessible to all board members via an intranet, a board-only Web site, or on demand. If the minutes refer to a budget, the book or the file should contain the budget document as well. The same is true for all other documents referenced in the minutes. The minutes book acts as a chronological record of all decisions and new or amended policies, when board members or officers were elected, and who was present at each meeting and how he or she voted on a specific issue. With an adequate recording of these facts, the board can remain confident that its board history is always within reach. The compilation should be available for legal review and can be used as a tool for board orientation. Minutes can also help absent board members stay on track and remain familiar with board decisions.

Q A member of our organization is requesting to see the last several minutes of board meetings. Are we obligated to give a copy?

A As always, check your state laws first to determine what they say about the members' right to review organizational documents. Your board meeting minutes are not necessarily public documents but members form a privileged group of stakeholders. In any case, ask the member why he would like to see the minutes. A justified reason certainly makes collaboration easier. If you get repeated requests from members, it makes sense to draft a policy on how to deal with this issue.

If a board is subject to sunshine laws, it most likely is required to publicly post its minutes. Each board should know what its state laws require. Some boards consider it a sign of transparency to share board meeting minutes with all constituents and post meeting minutes on their Web site. Sharing the minutes is one way to ensure that they are accurate, informative, and reflect properly on your board's priorities. Keep in mind, however, that confidential issues belong in an executive session.

RECORDING MEETINGS

Boards that record meetings should make sure that all board members are aware of the taping and that the pros and cons of this practice have been thoroughly weighed. Boards that deal with mounds of detailed information (e.g., foundation boards evaluating grant proposals or meetings where complicated financial transactions are discussed) may find it helpful to record the minutiae to facilitate the work of developing accurate minutes. The tape should not serve as the final record because it is not easily and quickly referenced.

On the other hand, a recorder may hinder open discussion and tame otherwise lively members from expressing their opinions for fear of comments being taken out of context or threat of personal liability. If a board uses tapes, a policy of how to deal with the tapes afterwards should be adopted. When are they destroyed and who may do it? A policy eliminates the risk of tapes being destroyed prematurely or by an unauthorized person who is intending to expunge possible evidence.

GENERATING BOARD REPORTS

Many standard board meeting agendas are inundated with reports: committee reports, the treasurer's report, and the chief executive's report. Clearly, reports have a role in meetings, but if they dominate a meeting, they focus the board on the past. As was previously suggested, standard board-related reports should be included in the consent agenda. The following section discusses the format and the purpose of these reports.

The main work of the board often happens in committees and task forces. These work groups are essential for getting the board's chores accomplished. The board delegates certain tasks or activities to these groups and usually expects to hear the results or progress at a future time. Without a common agreement on what the objective of these reports should be and how to best present the relevant data, reports may become filled with pages of unnecessary details and may be presented in numerous formats that make it difficult to track project advancement.

The purpose of a committee report is to

- keep the board informed on the evolution of a project

- communicate the results of a specific task that the committee undertook

- engage the board in discussion of an issue

- present recommendations for board action

If nothing has happened since the last meeting, no report is necessary. (Please see the committee report template in Appendix IV.)

The committee report is not the same as committee meeting minutes. The minutes are the record of what happened during the meeting; they mainly serve the committee's own purposes. Some committee meetings do not need official minutes; members simply keep notes for future reference and as an indication that the group has been in contact. The board does not need to know those details. It does however require a consolidated message (i.e., the report) that the group wants to confer to the rest of the board. Keep the minutes in the committee's own files.

It makes sense to develop a format for all committee reports or to at least set clear guidelines on what is relevant and essential. Using a standard software program or creating a template for committee members to complete can alleviate some of the work for the group's chair. Usually the committee or task-force chair is responsible for creating the report, preparing the meeting agenda, and ensuring that the committee's charge gets carried out.

COMMUNICATING ELECTRONICALLY BETWEEN MEETINGS

For most boards, it is imperative that activity continues between meetings and information and documents are shared. Minutes need to be circulated before the next session. Meeting planners need feedback on logistical issues. The chief executive should carry on continuous conversation with the chair and the rest of the board. The chair needs to follow up on board assignments. Some matters need not enter the boardroom and should be handled outside of official sessions.

Without a doubt, the electronic medium is the most efficient, cost-effective, and rapid way to communicate between meetings. However, there may still be individual board members who are not computer savvy or do not have the needed equipment. Fortunately, these cases are dwindling but they may still come up on boards that have "senior" members who do not use computers as their standard communication tools. If necessary, staff should be prepared to guide board members to locations where they can access a computer. This can include the organization's own offices, local affiliates, and public libraries. If there are some board members who simply are not able to take advantage of these facilities, the traditional methods of mailing or faxing materials and communicating via phone are tried and true solutions.

Here are some options for facilitating electronic communication between the senior staff and board and board members among themselves. Find the tools that work and fit the culture of your board.

- E-mail is the most common communication method. Documents can be shared and board members can suggest future agenda items. This is also a forum for members to share personal news with colleagues.

- A special section (portal or intranet) on the organization's Web site, accessible only to board members, allows you to archive needed and helpful documents and provide a permanent contact place where board members can go.

- A listserv or a chat room can be part of these structures to allow board members to communicate with each other in real time or over the course of time while keeping a permanent record. Electronic communication also helps overcome time zone differences.

- Blogs allow the chief executive to communicate how the organization is connected to and involved in the community. These blogs serve as an information tool for the board members as well as to keep them informed about issues important to the organization.

- Webinars serve a training purpose. Staff can conduct these sessions on specific topics and nobody needs to relocate for the purpose.

- LinkedIn networking under the organization's name can serve as a tool to share relevant articles, Web sites, or feedback on questions and discussion topics. This is not appropriate for sharing confidential information.

- Twitter may be a tool for some action-oriented committees to share ideas or quick updates on a project under way. Again, security issues may still be a concern and this communication method should not be used for internal board matters.

Because of the ease and rapid exchanges possible with e-mail and all Web-based communication, communication between board meetings is becoming less of a burden.

PROPER E-MAIL DECORUM

- Small-group discussions that exclude other board or committee members are not acceptable. Board-related messages are to be shared with everyone. It's as simple as using a group address and clicking on the "Reply All" button when sending or responding to an e-mail.

- Write a business e-mail only when you have something valuable to say. Be considerate about overloading your fellow members' inboxes.

- E-mails are not an excuse to use sloppy language and forget to check spelling. You are conveying professional and business information.

- Read the message one more time before hitting the send button.

- Don't convey confidential information via e-mail.

- Remember, there is a record of every message, so use personal e-mail addresses for personal messages.

REMEMBER

- Even if "laissez-faire" is your meeting motto, document everything carefully — before and after the meeting.

- Prepare your board members for a meeting by sending them relevant information at least a week before the meeting.

- Let your meeting agenda lead you to most effective use of time: Eliminate passivity from the meeting by adopting a consent agenda to incorporate more time for deliberation.

- Recapture the substance of your meeting in accurate minutes.

- Pay attention to in-between meeting communication. When addressing board issues, you are conducting business. Keep it relevant.

CASE STUDY
BETTER LATE THAN NEVER?

Ever since she joined the DEF board, Sue has attended every board meeting as well as her assigned committee meetings. But she is perpetually 20 to 30 minutes late to each one. She always apologizes profusely as she blows in, which is then followed by a minimum of five minutes of others saying, "Oh, it's OK, we understand, traffic is so difficult this time of day," etc. But board members are talking privately, saying they are growing tired of accommodating Sue's tardiness. Someone just might blow up at her one of these days!

Active participation in board meetings should be considered obligatory. When a board member arrives late, he or she misses key points of discussion and may find it impossible to be an active participant. Being on time for board meetings is expected — not just because it should be an understood obligation but also out of basic politeness and respect for everyone else's time.

If the tardiness is occasional, and the board member knows in advance that she will be late, she should

- let the board chair or another officer or member know that she will be late so that the meeting can go ahead and start without her

- refrain from commenting on business completed or in discussion prior to her arrival so that the team can move forward with the participants who have all the information

- follow up soon after the meeting with another board member to see what she missed

If the tardiness is chronic, something must be done to deal with it directly. Either the board chair or the governance committee chair needs to intervene and restate the expectation about being on time for board meetings.

If it is unclear what the real problem is, there is a possibility that the board member may be losing interest in the board's work. The board chair may wish to use this opportunity to determine if others are feeling the same way by leading a full board discussion about meetings in general and then making changes as needed.

- Are the meetings boring, badly prepared, or poorly chaired?

- Are all the meetings necessary?

- Are unimportant issues or "old business" first on the agenda?

- Are the meetings too long, held at an inconvenient time, or not scheduled enough in advance?

- Is the location of the meeting inconvenient?

Adapted from *Taming the Troublesome Board Member* by Katha Kissman, BoardSource, 2006.

CHAPTER 4

MEETING STRUCTURE, DECISION MAKING, AND VOTING

Q Our chair participates in all aspects of the meeting. Can he really make a motion? Or should he stay as a tie-breaker?

A Your chair did not lose his board member privileges when he was elected chair. He gained numerous additional duties — and even special powers — but his privileges did not change. Your chair is the facilitator of the meeting and that role is a demanding one. That does not give him the right to control the outcome of the discussions, but he still has a right to make his opinions known. A good chair listens and poses questions to keep the issues focused. He can also be an advocate by making a motion. Board members have a chance to second it — or not. The full board votes and determines the outcome of a motion.

How well board members carry out their duties, communicate with each other, work as a team, or solve problems are all closely related to the board's culture. These factors can either result in an efficient and productive team that works well together or as a dysfunctional and unproductive group. This chapter discusses the use of parliamentary procedure and explores a variety of decision-making and voting practices. It also looks at how a board's culture and structure affect the way that work is accomplished.

By looking at a board's processes in more detail, it is possible to determine whether it is a group hung up on procedures, functioning more as a private social club, or one that is continuously accomplishing something important. Running a meeting like a neighborhood social gathering is not the objective — no matter how enjoyable it can be. The board should meet for business reasons. Every board meeting should include some substantive matters that require the full attention of every member. If the environment is not conducive to business, haphazard decisions can result. If the culture of the board is too relaxed, it may be easy to step out of line and forget or ignore the legal aspects required for a board meeting.

For some boards, it may be helpful to set a dress code for board meetings. This can be communicated at a board member orientation or as part of casual conversation to new recruits. Whether it's business attire or more casual clothing, having everyone "fit in" eliminates any unnecessary judgment of a peer's importance or role on the board. However, board members should be sensitive to cultural, ethnic, and economic differences.

Every board needs some structure for its internal operations. Without structure there is no common reference to rely on when the unexpected happens. Specific standards serve as a guide to do the right thing, particularly when inappropriate board member behavior must be addressed. Standard practices help to bring clarity in dealing with disorder in the boardroom, with members who are habitually late, or even with illegible minutes. At the other end of the spectrum, too much structure and too many rules can stifle creativity and cause members to focus more on rules than results.

The most basic structural element of a business meeting is to start and end on time and this is the responsibility of the board chair. However, he or she cannot always control the comings and goings of individual board members unless the board culture has already stressed the importance of respecting the meeting's time frame. Board members often are busy people, running from appointment to appointment; or they are parents who must accommodate their children's schedules. It is common courtesy to stick to set time limits, show respect for private time, and allow board members to remain attentive to the rest of their lives.

A board has total freedom to choose its method for conducting its meetings, as long as all legal requirements and genuine ethical expectations are met. No state law nor federal law regulates the very detailed processes — or lack thereof — in a private business meeting. Fortunately, the choice to follow a strict parliamentary procedure or take a more relaxed approach is an internal decision. Some structure and order are necessary to keep proceedings from getting out of hand and to help guide the decision-making process.

BOARD STRUCTURE AND THE ROLE OF PARLIAMENTARY ORDER

Robert's Rules of Order is the most comprehensive, most widely used reference of meeting manuals. The original edition saw light in 1876; today, it is in its 10th edition. It is the most referenced meeting guide in the United States and appears as the referee in the bylaws of more nonprofits than we can manage to count. The detailed rules described in the book actually are best in a larger parliamentary setting, where the representatives determine what is best for their constituents who elected them (i.e., government representatives). Each representative does whatever is necessary to get his or her opinion accepted. It is standard and acceptable to represent a specific group and drive that group's agenda. Competition can be fierce between representatives of different opinions. It is important in that setting to follow rules and regulations so that everyone follows exactly the same procedures. Deviations may indicate that one side is being advantaged or disadvantaged. Exact process matters. If process did not exist, it would be easy to contest every unfavorable vote by referring to technicalities that are otherwise deemed unarguable by relying on procedure.

This atmosphere is (or should be) foreign to small nonprofit boards. Board members do not (or should not) act as representatives for a specific section of the organization's constituents and solely advocate its needs. They should certainly bring the understanding, wishes, and preferences of their groups into the boardroom, but only in the form of examples and testimonials of perspectives that the full board must consider when looking at the needs of the constituency at large. This principle does not mean that a board member should not have strong individual opinions on an issue. A variety of individual opinions brings diversity to the discussion and has an impact on how the final opinion of the board is formed. This understanding allows the board to focus on results and not get bogged down by process details as can happen in a true parliamentary setting. It provides flexibility that can be adapted to the culture of a board; it focuses on discussion and deliberation rather than on structuring every expression into a specific order.

A large number of nonprofit bylaws mention that board meetings are run according to *Robert's Rules of Order*. This can be seen as a good or bad thing. Without a doubt, the 700 pages of this "little" red book contain innumerable wisdoms and solutions to many sticky situations. They also spell out the exact steps for just about every boardroom event in detail. If the bylaws stipulate that Mr. Robert determines the board's processes, this notion cannot be selective. Either the rules are followed or the board should clarify its relationship with *Robert's Rules* in the bylaws.

A PARLIAMENTARIAN IN THE BOARDROOM

If a board includes a position for a parliamentarian to police the processes in the boardroom, it is likely taking a strict structure approach and may end up spending precious time discussing who is allowed to do what and when. If the purpose is to have a member who is able to guide an unwieldy board to respect order and provide professional assistance in a procedural situation that seemingly has no solution, a parliamentarian can be of help. If a meeting is very process oriented (which may be the case in some membership organizations), it is better to retain a parliamentarian to help only when necessary. This person does not need to be an organization insider.

By no means is this to say that structure and certain elements of parliamentary order should be eliminated from board meetings. Every meeting needs a frame, defined processes, and order. Without them — no matter how jolly and informal the atmosphere in the boardroom is — oligarchy or chaos can creep in. All parties might be speaking at the same time, the agenda would be difficult to follow, and the chair could lose control.

To avoid such chaos, at minimum: Check whether a quorum is present; declare the meeting started and adjourned; include motions, along with someone to second the motion; and allow the chair to facilitate discussion and make judgment calls when order is lost or unruly members dominate the floor. It is necessary to create a general understanding of what to do if an impasse happens and board members should be educated about the accepted processes and when they apply. Chairs need training in facilitation techniques to keep the team interconnected while respecting the members' right to express differing opinions.

When the chair leads the board through the agenda, the use of basic parliamentary order keeps business moving forward. Using motions, board members can bring in issues for discussion. This facilitates tracking and recording. But when a major discussion is launched, the most flexible and probably productive method is to rely on the chair's skills in facilitation. Deliberation can be guided by the chair with a more free-flowing manner that invites open contemplation and creative solutions. When the chair judges that all opinions have been aired and that the group is ready for a vote, he or she may then put the motions back on the table and record the voting results.

If a board chooses to have a professional meeting reference guidebook, such as *Robert's Rules of Order,* it should first study some available books and documents and choose the reference that most closely fits the board's comfort level. (Check the Suggested Resources at the end of this book for further ideas, and have a task force make a recommendation.) A board should determine what parliamentary order means to it and indicate in the bylaws how it plans to use the reference. To include flexibility in the processes, the bylaws could state that the reference serves as a tool to solve a bottleneck when the board is not able to agree on a process issue through direct communication. Legal counsel should interpret the board's intent. Here is one example:

In case of an impasse or in a situation that cannot be solved via discussion, the board relies on the guidance of *Robert's Rules of Order* [or another reference of choice].

Q We are mandated by a state health care agency to hold board meetings every month. We are also mandated to keep the board abreast of what is going on. We do that by drafting a monthly report in which each department report is integrated. This has evolved into a very boring exercise and has made it a chore for everyone to come to board meetings. How can we, under these conditions, make our meetings more relevant?

A No surprise that your meetings are boring! If they involve only reading and listening to operational reports, it would be a surprise to see smiling, eager members at your meetings.

Try to change the focus of the meetings. By concentrating on the past, the board is not — or does not even have a chance of — doing its share to lead the organization in the right direction. Even with a complicated mandated structure, your board should be able to focus on the future.

Designate a person to compile the report. Create guidelines for things to include. Do not feed your board details that it should not worry about. Massage the report (maybe include a dashboard compilation) to reflect the overall big picture that should interest the board. Make the presentation captivating with charts, color, and pictures. If you send your reports ahead of time, they can be read and digested outside of the meeting. As a result, your board will find new time in the meeting where it can get involved in issues that it should think about.

USING DELIBERATION IN DECISION MAKING

As already discussed, meetings need overall structure. Without any structure there is chaos. For a board that thrives on rules and repetitive framework, some level of parliamentary order may provide the desired frame for meetings. But certain parts of a meeting can always benefit from a more laid-back approach. The board chair can announce when the meeting suspends parliamentary rules and moves to deliberation. Then the chair can guide the discussion without having to incorporate motions and other details into the process. When it is clear that the board is ready to make a decision, the chair announces that the deliberation part is over and the regular process takes over.

Deliberation drives good decisions; it is the meat and bones of a meeting. During deliberation, members of the board discuss all sides of an issue. Without a thorough airing of all aspects relating to the issue under discussion, it is difficult to end up with a conclusion that is sound, founded, and fair.

The following is a basic outline for the chair to conduct the deliberation process and to use deliberation time constructively. Board members should have prepared for the meeting by defining the pros and cons ahead of time. The left column outlines the process while the right column provides an example of how deliberation works. In this case, the board of a youth service organization is discussing options for program collaboration with other organizations. To prepare, the program director wrote a report to frame the issue and sent it to board members so they could come to the meeting ready to discuss the pros and cons of the issue.

PROCESS FOR DELIBERATION

Steps in the Process	Process for Youth Organization Board
1. Chair explains items to be discussed. • Introduce the topic in the most neutral way possible. • State the key points, define the dilemma, and clarify why this issue is important or why the board needs to address it.	1. Chair reminds the board what collaboration means to the organization: opportunities, losses, challenges.
2. State what needs to be accomplished. • Define the objectives and make sure that everybody is in agreement. • Frame the issue carefully to eliminate contention.	2. Chair reminds everyone that this is a preliminary discussion. The board does not have to make a final decision immediately.
3. Lead a discussion. • Encourage open discussion (concerns, missing issues, new ideas, controversies).	3. Chair invites everyone to state pros and cons of collaboration. • Local competition for the same clients • Cutting costs and expanding scope After discussion, the board leans toward collaboration. • If we do not move ahead, someone else will take our place. • We will be able to serve more young people by diversifying our programs.
4. Search for solutions and options for action. • Ask for feedback. • Ask for alternative solutions. • Look for mission connection. • Assess need for resources.	4. Set up a task force to study existing proposals more closely; include the chief executive. Report at next meeting.

Another approach during deliberation is to rely on so-called systems thinking. The chair will identify the issue or problem under discussion. He or she proceeds by posing guiding questions that lead to a better understanding of the ripple effects of various options. Ultimately, it is easier to consider possible actions because the board members have a deeper appreciation of the full implications of the decision. This process requires the chair to be able to guide the discussion fairly by asking relevant questions.

Using small groups during the deliberation process is a great way of directly involving every board member. Small groups can more efficiently discuss various aspects of the same issue. The board can divide bigger issues into smaller increments, task the smaller groups with discussing the issue, and then report back to the board with their ideas. Small groups also allow for more focused reflection and provide more opportunities for less vocal members to make a contribution to the deliberation process.

Without an open and careful study of the details that make up a case, one can end up relying on wishful thinking rather than on facts and experience. A diversified board that brings a variety of opinions and expertise to the discussion has a better chance of guiding the organization in the right direction — a responsibility that weighs heavily on every board member's shoulders.

REACHING A UNANIMOUS DECISION

Most nonprofit bylaws indicate that the majority voice of a quorum carries the vote, while issues of special importance may need a supermajority. Unanimity can be a blessing if it is achieved through a thoughtful process when the issue has been analyzed from all sides. But it also comes with caveats and may indicate internal problems. With everyone always in full agreement, it may mean that the board is simply rubberstamping recommendations. It could imply that only the noncontroversial aspects of an issue were aired, and that no one took the time to do complete research, or that the board is composed of similarly thinking individuals who prefer a one-sided story. A habitually unanimous board may not realize that disagreement actually stimulates thinking and elevates discussion to a different level. If unanimity seems to be a pattern, it may be time for the board to investigate some of the reasons behind it. Under all circumstances, it is important to remind everyone that board decisions are communicated without dissent to the outside world.

SEEKING CONSENSUS

Consensus is another approach for making decisions. Seeking consensus — a general agreement to a proposed idea — is not always well understood because it is a complicated process. It demands a skillful facilitator and requires that the board fully understand the consensus-building process. Consensus building may be the most democratic way of coming to a final accord, although it may not be an easy or quick way to run a board meeting.

The principle of consensus building assumes that all points of view are valid and incorporate minority views into the discussion. The goal is to find a solution that everyone can accept and is willing to implement. Consensus eliminates the win-or-lose approach of a majority vote because it does not count votes. It takes a qualitative approach, not forcing a compromise but seeking to eliminate objections. It also encourages alternative thinking and fosters innovative solutions.

During the process, the facilitator presents a proposal and invites all participants to express their concerns or reservations. This input may result in a modification of the proposal, gradually allowing it to become more and more specific. Modification moves from major points to fine-tuning the final agreement. Prioritizing points is a useful way of eliminating unacceptable solutions. Synthesizing opinions brings clarification to concepts. When the facilitator feels that a mutual agreement has been reached, this is articulated and the chair asks if participants agree that the articulated statement accurately reflects the consensus. If there is no objection, it is recorded as the group's decision.

PITFALLS OF CONSENSUS PROCESS

- Unaccustomed participants without proper training can keep others as prisoners of the process.

- Without a skilled facilitator, the process may have difficulties reaching conclusion.

- Someone's lack of patience can ruin the atmosphere and others' spirits.

- Final decisions may seem diluted to some.

- Board meetings may last longer that anticipated.

The consensus method may not be practical for all board decisions because of its cumbersome and time-consuming aspect, but it could be used for highly sensitive, risky, or ethical issues that the board must tackle, such as determining a desired profile for the board or deciding on a stand the board wants to take on a controversial environmental issue. A consensus may not always be reached. A small fraction of the board can block action that might be desired by the majority of members. A deadlock may happen if a board member is unwilling or unable to accept the principle of the method itself. In these situations, the objection must be worked out before the proposal can go forward. Ultimately, a totally new approach to the question at hand may be necessary and the full process must start all over again.

HOW DO BOARDS VOTE?

In most cases, deliberation (or whatever method the board uses to get ready for decision making or the final agreement) results in a vote. By casting a vote, each board member expresses his or her personal assessment of the situation and thus contributes to collective decision making. However, it is only the collective vote that counts at the end.

Whether a board votes by a show of hands or by voice is up to the board. The size of the board may determine the method. There is no right or wrong way of voting as long as the secretary is able to count the votes and can ascertain who voted for and who voted against. It is unusual for a board to vote by ballot. Ballots are more common and practical for membership meetings where larger groups are present, and only the final count matters. (Please see sample ballots in Appendix V.)

Openness is an element of board interaction. It demands that board members trust and understand each other as votes are cast according to their best judgment. If opinions on the substance of the issue under consideration are openly shared during deliberation, it is easier to eliminate the sense of voting "against" a colleague. Some boards use a secret ballot when electing officers. The purpose of this is to eliminate any adverse impact on relationships when a choice has to be made between two peers.

Future board leadership is at stake when new officers are nominated. To eliminate natural pressure from officer elections, it may make sense to have the governance committee act as a facilitator for the process. In this case, the governance committee holds discreet conversations with officer candidates outside of the boardroom. Committee members are able to confidentially communicate with officer candidates and other board members and then present for confirmation one candidate.

A few states allow nonprofit boards to vote via electronic means but require a clear process to make the vote legally binding. Minnesota is one of the forerunners. In Minnesota, nonprofit boards that choose to use electronic voting must be able to create a record that can be retained, retrieved, and reviewed. Board members must agree in writing to carry out board action without a meeting. It is important to authenticate the actual consent when a vote takes place, as it is always possible for outsiders to log in. Presently at least Texas, Virginia, Wisconsin, Utah, Minnesota, and Washington, D.C., have endorsed the use of electronically scanned signatures for electronic board meetings. For truly sensitive e-mails, it is possible to encrypt message contents so that only authorized recipients are able to open them. Privacy issues are in danger if proper precautions are not taken.

In California, a 2005 law allows board members to vote electronically under the following conditions:

- All board members provide unanimous written consent.

- This permission can be withdrawn any time.

- E-mail addresses must be verified if a meeting notice is sent electronically.

- All board members must be able to be present electronically at the same time.

- All votes must have a record for inspection.

DECIDING BY MAJORITY RULE

Most state laws require that a majority of the board members present (after a quorum is determined) must agree before a vote is carried. A majority means 51 percent — or, if there are 10 voting members present, six will carry the vote. The justification for this law, again, is to ensure that there is a reasonable agreement among board members on the desired outcomes of a vote.

Majority rule usually refers to normal board decisions. Bylaws should distinguish between "normal" and "extraordinary" decisions. They should clarify what kinds of major resolutions — ones that have a foremost impact on the board or the entire organization — should require a greater than majority vote. A small part of the board should not be able to decide whether to shut down the organization, approve a merger, amend the articles of incorporation or the bylaws, fire the chief executive, or remove a board member or an officer. It is common to require a two-thirds or three-quarters vote on these issues.

A board can also agree ahead of time on what kinds of decisions demand deliberation, when a simple majority is enough, when the board must rely on a higher level of agreement, or when the board does not even need to address the issue. For example:

- A conceptual amendment to a bylaws clause must be discussed and a supermajority must pass it.

- To confirm a new address in the same document is a technicality; this proposal can be included in the consent agenda that gets voted by majority rule.

- Firing a chief executive should be deliberated by the full board with a high degree of consent needed.

- Deciding to use an executive search firm can be determined by a majority during a normal course of the meeting.

- Determining the keynote speaker at the next conference does not need to reach the boardroom. The chief executive can approve the choice and the good news will be shared with the board.

- Approval of the staff compensation item in the budget is a board decision, but the chief executive determines the actual distribution of the funds among staff members. (Caveat: The board should approve the senior staff total compensation as they appear in the Form 990.)

- The full board also approves — and hopefully unanimously — the chief executive's compensation package.

- The bylaws may give the chair the right to decide on who chairs each committee.

- The chair and the chief executive together decide the contents of the meeting agenda.

VOTING BY PROXY

State law often defines whether a nonprofit board may use proxy votes. A proxy generally refers to either the person with a power of attorney, or the piece of paper that conveys this power to vote or make decisions on behalf of a board member in his or her absence. This practice is commonly used by for-profit corporations and nonprofit membership organizations during membership meetings. Under those circumstances it can be highly beneficial and useful as it allows for adequate representation when bringing together thousands of shareholders or members is impractical. However, for nonprofit boards, proxy voting is generally not a good practice.

State laws that address this issue agree with this notion. Why? A board member is accountable for his or her own actions on the board. Because of liability issues, a board member is not in a good position to delegate major responsibilities to someone else. A board member must adhere to the duty of care as the fiduciary of the organization's assets and well-being. Careful decision making is more than simply agreeing or disagreeing with a proposal.

Most board decisions are not simple yes or no votes. If that were the case, it would be easy to share basic documents with board members and ask them to indicate whether they are for or against the issue. So why even bother to come to the meeting? Because it is impossible to know ahead of time what the true issues are in the minds of the other board members. During deliberation a point may come up that could turn the tables. A board member indicating opposition to a proposal in a proxy might change his or her mind after hearing the arguments. A proxy can lock in a vote prematurely.

MANAGING SPLIT VOTES

If board members regularly feel incompatible and divisive, there must be an underlying systemic reason. Few boards are unanimous all the time — and if they are, it leaves room for question.

For small boards, a constant split vote may indicate that the board cannot absorb differing opinions and reach consensus. One or two individuals veering off the mainstream can create a split vote. The solution may be to elevate board member recruitment to the top of the board's priority list. This will help build a larger member base that can contribute to information sharing and that is able to analyze all questions carefully. It may also make sense to discuss the goals and vision for the organization and verify that everyone is still on the same page about how to reach them.

Power struggles and cliques tend to lead to divisiveness. Private agendas often guide members' opinions and winning a debate becomes the objective. Board members can forget that they are part of an important team whose role is to lead the organization forward. Differing opinions can be a blessing during a deliberation process, but working toward a consensus or a compromise is also part of a democratic process. If cliques or competing factions define the board composition, it may be necessary to eliminate this obstacle. If board members are not able to solve this serious problem on their own, it may be valuable to invite an outside facilitator to help iron out the stumbling block through the use of conflict resolution techniques.

Occasional split votes are to be expected. This can happen with controversial issues or when the topic has not yet been researched or analyzed thoroughly. It can also happen when board members simply react with their deep personal conviction concerning an issue or when a personal experience does not allow them to deviate from their initial perspective. Additional time or work on the issue may be all that is needed, or the chair may attempt to rephrase the debated issue to make it more palatable and acceptable to more board members.

Without having to rely on the chair to break a tie (see page 69 for "Should the Chair Vote?"), a more constructive approach would be to test different decision-making processes that have been outlined earlier in this chapter. Even if the bylaws require a majority rule to carry the vote, the board may benefit from trying the following:

- Encourage more early information sharing.

- Attempt consensus building with the board.

- Restate the issue using different words.

- Ask all board members to carefully elaborate on the obstacles that they see ahead of them and what measures would turn the issue around in their minds.

All of these efforts expect that board members are familiar with their duty of loyalty, place personal needs in proper perspective, and understand and accept their collective role in defining what the organizational needs are.

ABSTAINING FROM VOTING

Do board members have the right — the moral right — not to express their opinion when no apparent conflicting or logistical reason exists? Should board members ever shy away from controversial or otherwise tough decisions? Is voting an obligation or a privilege in the boardroom setting? These are challenging questions, and it is difficult to propose a stock answer.

While abstention is usually tied to a conflict of interest — and is expected under such circumstances — sometimes board members do not vote because they remain undecided (often corrected by further discussion). In some cases, a board member may not want to cast an unpopular vote or vote against another peer. This could be construed as having "undue" influence or voting with the pack. Rubberstamping boards often let strong leaders guide their opinions.

Abstention can produce two kinds of results: It can prevent a majority from carrying the vote, or it can allow the final decision to swing to the minority because of lack of sufficient and determined support. If a board is clearly divided and time allows it, the best solution may be to table the issue until the next meeting and assign a task force to address the issue in between the meetings.

Q In a recent vote, we had three yeses and three no's and one abstention. So what was the final result?

A If your abstaining board member has a conflict of interest, he was correct not to vote. If he simply was undecided, you have a trickier situation to deal with.

It is not always easy to be a board member. At times, you find yourself in a situation where you may have to vote against your peers, your mentors, your favorite colleagues, or against the recommendations of the chief executive. As a board member, you are expected to make independent decisions and come to conclusions that reflect your personal feelings and convictions about what is best for the organization under the circumstances. If you are expecting a controversial issue to come up for a vote, do your own due diligence ahead of time. Study the issue, talk to those who might be affected by the results; and, in the board meeting, participate in deliberation, information sharing, and debate.

Not all decisions are easy, but being a board member sometimes takes bravery. If board members abstained every time they were uncomfortable about opposing someone else or truly expressing their opinions on major issues, they probably should reconsider their service on that board.

You can't force anyone to vote, so this may be more of an issue of the board discussing what abstentions might mean to it. There are probably different ways to look at the impact of abstentions. An abstention vote might be counted among the no's and in that case, your vote did not go through. More often an abstention vote is considered an agreement with the majority. As you did not have a majority, your chair might either vote or abstain from voting: that could help decide the case in this situation.

REMEMBER

- Too much order or too much casualness may compromise your meeting efficiency. Find the right balance for your culture to support the board's role and functions.

- Reaching a decision is one of the primary goals in most meetings. Test different decision-making models to find the one that helps bring the best results during your board meetings.

- Whatever your choice of process is, embrace thorough deliberation before making a decision.

- Assess ahead of time for which issues a majority rule is not adequate and requires even tighter agreement among all members.

- Set the right tone: Start and end on time.

CASE STUDY
SILENCE IS NOT ALWAYS GOLDEN

Jeff was well respected and admired by his board colleagues — and for good reason. Whenever he offered his input in a discussion, it was always very clear and well thought out. Usually, whatever he had to say was one of the most valuable pieces of information the board received about any given topic. Unfortunately, Jeff did not always contribute to discussions. In fact, there were often two or three meetings in a row where Jeff never said a word!

Board members are brought on the board to contribute their ideas and expertise. Unfortunately, when a member does not participate in discussions, the rest of the board misses out on his or her potentially valuable knowledge and insight. Then, in the rare occasion when that person does speak up, his or her voice may be too quickly overlooked or dismissed. Ultimately, a silent board member is taking the place of someone else who could be more active on the board.

There are many possible reasons for a board member's hesitation to speak out during board meetings. This person may feel any of the following:

- insecurity or discomfort when speaking in public

- the contributions of others are more worthwhile than his or her own

- everything that should be said has been said already

- others are dominating the discussion to such an extent that the person doesn't want to compete

It may be beneficial for the board chair to have an informal, one-on-one conversation with the quiet board member. Whether this person is holding back due to dominating board members or a big-picture concern regarding the board or organization as a whole, it's necessary for the board chair to know what the issues are and do something about them. If, however, it is a matter of shyness or passivity, the board chair should reassure the board member that his or her contribution is absolutely necessary, wanted, and valued, and then find ways to draw participation out of each and every board member. Simple presence is not enough in the boardroom.

The board chair could and should make it a point to require group discussion at each meeting, literally going around the room and asking each person to share thoughts, concerns, or suggestions.

Additionally, providing board members with the tools to make personal insights, such as the Myers-Briggs Type Indicator, would also be helpful. This is a good exercise for each board member individually and for the team as a whole, so that board members get to know one another on a more personal level and gain a better understanding of how each person works best in a group atmosphere. Sometimes the necessary give and take in the boardroom is something that requires careful observation, personal understanding, and finesse.

Adapted from *Taming the Troublesome Board Member* by Katha Kissman, BoardSource, 2006.

CHAPTER 5

MEETING PARTICIPATION

Q Should we go ahead with our board meeting even though the chief executive is not able to attend?

A Considering the importance of the chief executive, it would be unfortunate to miss her input. However, as long as quorum is reached, the meeting can proceed. If the chief executive is a nonvoting member, her presence does not affect the quorum.

In the case where the chief executive cannot attend the meeting, the board chair should take it upon him-or herself to communicate with the executive afterwards and provide good feedback on what happened at the meeting. If there are some decisions on the table that absolutely require the chief executive's input or greatly benefit from it, the board might either include the executive via teleconference, or if possible, postpone the discussion or final decision until the next meeting.

In this chapter we look at the people who participate in a board meeting along with guidelines for their participation and rules for meeting attendance. These participants can animate a board meeting or cause it to drag on interminably. Some attendees should be present from beginning to end, and others appear only at critical moments. Some participants lead the show in the meeting room; others prepare for the meeting before and after. Clarifying the expectations of every person affiliated with a board meeting simply ensures that unnecessary confusion is absent and that the right individuals are chosen for the appropriate roles.

How to consolidate all these expectations? By looking at all the aspects that influence the atmosphere and desired outcomes of the meeting, it is possible to start isolating the factors that make this possible.

A committed board member	• wants to feel that his or her time is well spent and contributions are appreciated.
	• wants the chair to conduct the meeting in a capable manner and other members to express valid and relative comments on the issue under discussion.
	• wants to get excited about the work and the accomplishments of the organization and leave invigorated and with anticipation of the next meeting.
A committed chair	• wants an orderly meeting with active participants.
	• welcomes unconventional comments that stimulate discussion and force even the quiet ones to express their opinions.
	• wants to follow the agenda and expects clear and committed decisions at the end.
A committed chief executive	• looks forward to interacting with the full board as a team.
	• wants a board that understands the challenges with which he or she must struggle every day.
	• wants to feel that the board is behind him or her, supporting efforts and providing clear and unambiguous guidance for future actions.

NO QUORUM, NO MEETING

Before we discuss in more detail the various flexibilities and incentives boards use to get members to come together and make weighty decisions for their organizations, we need to understand one crucial legal requirement for a valid board meeting: a quorum. State corporation laws set quorum requirements to ensure that board decisions actually are made by elected board members!

A quorum defines how many board members must be in the room before a meeting can begin. No board meeting can take place without a quorum. If there is no quorum, the group that has gathered cannot make decisions and must adjourn and schedule its next meeting. Many state laws set a quorum as a majority of voting board members if the bylaws do not define other standards. If the bylaws mention nothing about a quorum, then state law prevails. Quorum should, however, be defined in the bylaws.

Why is a quorum required? Consider the following situation: A board with nine members has a meeting set for a Thursday evening. It is a stormy night and only the chair and another officer manage to come to the meeting. The two vote to remove three of their fellow members and assign to themselves a signature authority for all checks over $200.

This is an exaggerated example, but it makes a point: A quorum ensures that one or just a few board members do not make decisions without the board's consent.

It is always useful to contemplate the worst-case scenarios when defining decision-making quorum standards for the board. Combining a bad quorum definition with a majority rule can also spell disaster. For example, a board with 16 members and a 40 percent quorum requirement means that a minimum of six people is required for a vote. In this case, four members (a majority of the six in attendance) can determine the fate of an issue.

Some boards struggling with board member absenteeism may consider lowering the quorum because it seems impossible to get anything done. This is an approach that, ultimately, tries to correct a bad situation with a worse remedy, sending the wrong message to members about their obligation to attend meetings. Boards that set the quorum at 100 percent, hoping to ensure full representation, may find themselves in the same dilemma because, oftentimes, at least one member is absent from a meeting for a good reason.

In the end, simple presence, unfortunately, does not suffice. Active participation should also be considered obligatory. Counting heads and meeting quorum requirements allows the board to function within the legal parameters. But, as already mentioned, legality builds a necessary framework and gives the board the permission to act; it does not provide wisdom and ultimate personal accountability. Involvement in deliberation (asking questions, providing feedback, sharing ideas, or refusing to accept easy solutions) builds the needed base for wise decisions. After all, is that not the purpose for coming together?

THE ABSENTEE BOARD MEMBER

When a person accepts an invitation to serve on a board, his or her number one obligation is to come to meetings. Additionally, board service comes with the caveat of personal liability, which involves prudent and independent decision making. Without discussion and informed voting, a board member is not acting as a fiduciary for the organization. Absence endangers a member's capacity to be educated and to inform others.

But it is only natural that from time to time a board member will miss a meeting. When this happens, the member should communicate the excuse to the chair. It is inappropriate to just not show up. If members have marked the year's meeting dates in their calendars, only exceptional and unavoidable excuses should be acceptable: illness, family misfortune, or logistical causes beyond a member's control. When missing a meeting is unavoidable, it may be possible to participate via teleconference.

ADDRESSING ABSENCE FROM MEETINGS IN THE BYLAWS

Be aware of clauses in the bylaws concerning absenteeism. Some bylaws automatically consider a board member resigned after missing a certain number of meetings during a year or consecutively. Below are some sample bylaws clauses. Consider carefully what kind of phrasing is appropriate for your board.

1. Any elected officer or board member who is absent from two (2) consecutive regular meetings during a single administrative year shall automatically vacate the seat and vacancy shall be filled as provided by the bylaws. However, the board considers each absence as a separate circumstance and may expressly waive such absence by affirmative vote of a majority of its members.

2. Absence from three (3) consecutive board meetings within a fiscal year without excuse is equivalent to resignation from the board. Confirmation of such absences and subsequent removal shall be given to the board member in writing by the secretary of the board.

3. Any director may be removed by a two-thirds (2/3) vote of a quorum whenever, in the board's judgment, the best interest of the corporation would be served. Notice of the removal shall be given in writing to the board member by the secretary not more than ten (10) days subsequent to such action.

4. Board members who miss two (2) consecutive meetings shall be asked to resign.

A prolonged absence or missing several meetings in a row deserves attention. Probably the most common reason for board members to regularly miss meetings is lack of interest — their concern is just no longer there. The member may feel that he or she has done all that is possible. However, these feelings can be very difficult to communicate. The board member may feel like giving up or that he or she is letting others down. When a board member starts missing meetings, it is up to the chair to pick up the phone and simply ask: "What's up?" If the reason is the one described above, the call may be the saving grace. This is an opportunity for the disinterested individual to explain why he or she has lost interest or to communicate why he or she is too busy to continue. If there is no way to turn the situation around, the chair may need to ask the board member to officially resign. This is the most civilized way to handle a perfectly natural situation. It provides a dignified way out while reserving the possibility to keep the person involved in another capacity that does not require the same commitment.

By contacting a missing board member, the chair may learn that there are personal problems that have prevented regular attendance. The reason may be health related, a family matter, or a delicate, private subject that the board member may not even want to divulge. In this situation, the chair is often asked to demonstrate special sensitivity and skills in dealing with the situation in the most appropriate manner possible. Trust may be the key to reach the right solution, and confidentiality is crucial. Sometimes the right approach is to ask the board member to resign for the time being and, if the situation improves, he should feel welcome to apply for board membership again.

If the reasons for absence are a bad match between the member and the board, or that the expectations of the job were far different than the realities, the chair should request an official resignation. The chair may also wish to remain in touch in order to perhaps involve this person in the mission via other methods.

If the reasons for absence are uninspiring meetings or failure to use or take advantage of the skills of the member, the chair should get the message. There is a danger of possibly losing a valuable board member because the board was not functioning up to par. The chair should be able to listen and validate the board member's concerns and make the necessary efforts to correct the problems.

Logistics, as discussed previously, can also be a reason for low attendance. Be it transportation issues, child-care needs, timing of the meetings, or other reasons, the easiest way to solve this problem is to encourage board members to divulge the reason before it turns into an obstacle. Transportation and child care can be arranged, and meeting schedules can often be adjusted. By simply presenting them to the board, many other practical issues may be easily and creatively worked out.

LEAVE OF ABSENCE

Some boards, either as a precautionary measure or after being confronted with a situation, draft policies concerning leaves of absence. Should a board consider temporary absence acceptable, or should it deal with the issue more strictly? Requests for leave may warrant thorough consideration by the board. A board member may need to be absent for several months due to health issues or travel obligations and be unable to attend meetings or fulfill other board responsibilities. At least two options are available: (1) The board may demand that the member resign while still allowing him or her a request a chance to return for service when the situation has cleared itself, or (2) the board may have a policy that allows members to take a leave of absence under dire circumstances and relieves them of duties for the necessary period.

If the latter option is the choice, both the board and the board member in question need to ensure that proper precautions are in place. The board may want to draft a policy that specifically states the acceptable circumstances for a leave of absence. There is no reason to consider a sabbatical when a board member simply "wants to take a break" or has other temporary priorities for his or her time. Automatic sabbaticals are not a good idea either, as they undermine the basic commitment of board service. The minutes must reflect the dates of absence in order to protect the board member from liability. Keep the member informed about what happened during his or her absence by sharing documents, minutes, and board resolutions. (Please see a sample resolution in Appendix VI.) This is a cautionary measure meant to bring the member up to date on board business before returning to service. A vigilant board member might check with his or her own legal counsel of possible considerations that otherwise may go unnoticed. Only a lawyer can assess whether all liability issues have been addressed in the agreement.

GOVERNANCE COMMITTEE TAKES CHARGE!

The two important functions of a governance committee are to help build a competent and committed board and to ensure that the necessary tools and guidance are at the reach of the board to facilitate its job. The governance committee can support the chair and help elevate the quality of board meetings by

- keeping its eyes and ears open during meetings to detect process problems and challenges and finding solutions to them

- paying attention to attendance in meetings, and if it lags, figuring out ways to improve it

- brainstorming potential tips or tools to help meetings run more smoothly

- sketching board development moments for meetings

- serving as a neutral contact point for board members who do not feel comfortable going to the chair or the chief executive with their meeting issues or questions

- administering meeting evaluations on a regular basis to ensure improvements take place (Please see sample meeting evaluation forms in Appendix VII.)

- taking a leading role in organizing orientation sessions and board retreats

OTHER PARTICIPANTS IN MEETINGS

Besides the core — individual board members — the boardroom may fill up with numerous other participants without whom it would be difficult to conduct a productive meeting. Let's look at these roles in more detail.

THE BOARD CHAIR

It is difficult to imagine an efficient meeting without a designated facilitator or leader. During board meetings, this role usually falls on the shoulders of the chair. (When the chair is not available, the vice chair steps in. Running the meeting in the absence of the chair is one of the main duties of a vice chair, but the board may also elect a temporary or pro tem chair.) However, there is no law that says that the chair must preside over the meeting, even if the title seems to indicate so. If the chair is brilliant in all other ways but simply runs a lousy meeting, the board may consider assigning this task to someone else. While doing so may seem to indicate a lack of confidence in the chair leadership qualities, that is not always the case. Boards require articulate, decisive facilitators who are in total control of all situations. A board should choose the best facilitator, and with luck, that person is the chair. If not, it does not make sense to sacrifice the quality of the meeting because of tradition.

The role of the chair (we assume here that the board chair is presiding) is to make sure that the agenda fits the meeting and that the meeting runs smoothly. The chair ensures that board members are assuming their roles and responsibilities. During the meeting the chair facilitates the proceedings and discussion, and promotes civility during the debate. This demands a basic knowledge of parliamentary order, even if the board does not adhere to strict parliamentary procedure. The chair also is expected to have completed the necessary preparations for addressing the big issues of the meeting without having decided ahead of time what the outcome should be. All of these expectations mean that the chair has the skill to engage every member in the discussion — to tame the wild ones and encourage the quiet ones.

It is up to the chair to ensure that the objectives in the agenda are achieved. A good agenda allows for some flexibility, and a skillful chair knows when to utilize that flexibility. If one of the main issues simply demands more attention than anticipated, the chair should judge whether the discussion should continue, or if it is advisable to keep to the schedule and send the issue to committee for further study, bringing it back at the next meeting.

The chair's role does not end when the meeting does. There must be continued communication with the chief executive and with board members who are assigned special tasks. The chair is in the best position — better than the chief executive — to check on peers and ensure that everyone will come back with the appropriate work done. As a good practice, the chair should make a quick call or send an e-mail a few weeks prior to the next meeting to check on the status of the assignments. The chair should also contact board members who missed the last meeting, sending a message that she cares and wants every member present every time.

QUALITIES OF A GOOD MEETING FACILITATOR

The chair can rely on numerous tested principles to facilitate a productive meeting:

- Know board members thoroughly — what personal attributes they can contribute and who is in need of special attention.

- Own the agenda. The chair should be familiar with the items and seek a wide range of opinions.

- Explain any personal philosophies of running meetings to members in order to create a mutual understanding of what is acceptable and where the limits lie.

- Engage every board member during the meeting. Don't let the timid escape or the tired sleep.

- Control the domineering characters. Do not let the verbose members dominate the floor. Try to bring the best out of even the difficult colleagues.

- Remain objective and fair. Let controversial issues and opinions come out. Don't let personal opinions influence facilitation.

- Be familiar with basic meeting procedures. Know the conventional process and when to safely break from the conventional.

- Even if the chair is part of the group, in the facilitator capacity the chair must function as a neutral leader to earn the respect of peers.

- Use humor in the boardroom. If it does not come naturally, study ways to relax the atmosphere. There is no law dictating that board meetings must be stiff and boring.

Board meetings follow a continual cycle, leaving little rest for the board chair. The position of board chair is not limited to a call to order and adjournment. It involves regular preparation and follow-up, and takes a special commitment to the other members of the board — and the job itself.

STAYING FOCUSED ON THE RIGHT ISSUES

Disorderly and unstructured discussions can often be attributed to the chair's lack of skills. The chair has the gavel — literally or figuratively — to guide the discussion and participants. A good facilitator is able to keep the participants in line, engaged, and interested; follow the agenda; assess when additional time is warranted for a topic; and determine when the issue has been sufficiently discussed. The chair also directs the cadence and content of the debate.

Many boards include members who seem to have a need to perform. They must comment on every question. If the chair is not able to limit their delivery, the direction of the discussion can become lopsided, steering the board off on a tangent that may not be relevant or that receives exaggerated attention. To correct this, the chair may want to develop rules for how long every board member may speak. The board might want to elect a timekeeper or another member who raises a red flag when time is up. The chair can also limit the number of times a board member may speak during the meeting in order to leave time for the quieter members or those who need more time to think before expressing their opinions.

The chair must also be able to determine when everything has been said and it is time to vote. Or, if it is impossible to reach consensus, the chair has the right to table the discussion, if the issue allows, and bring it back during the next session after tempers have cooled and additional data are available. In this situation, the chair's decisiveness and good judgment allow the meeting to proceed.

The agenda is the best tool for the chair to maintain focus on the debate. The agenda is the recipe for the meeting, and including the appropriate and timely issues in the agenda can eliminate irrelevance. However, a carefully planned board meeting agenda must be flexible. The chair and the chief executive may need to turn the tables around and restructure the meeting altogether on short notice or, at least, insert a vital item between regular issues. This reflects responsibility and responsiveness and communicates to the rest of the board that they are on top of the issues.

SHOULD THE CHAIR VOTE?

Many boards struggle with the question of whether the board chair should vote during the meeting. Let's not forget that voting rights do extend to the chair, as he or she has the same rights as every other board member. It is up to each individual board chair to determine how he or she wants to use this right. It might make sense, when a new chair takes office, to bring up the issue and discuss his or her approach during the tenure. If there is no overall acknowledgment on this practice, usually the board's custom prevails.

As the facilitator of the meeting, the chair potentially has a chance to influence the free flow of opinions or ensure that a particular angle gets preferred visibility. A fair chair is aware of this and uses the facilitator role in an objective manner. The chair's vote can be very influential particularly in a small board where ties are common. It is important, therefore, that the chair remains impartial during deliberation, without promoting his own opinion. But at the end, the chair may simply vote with the rest of the board members. Should the chair have a particularly strong opinion on an issue, he or she may choose to temporarily delegate the role of facilitator to another board member while discussion takes place. This enables the chair to contribute to the discussion and offer important insight and direction without appearing to sway the discussion in a particular direction. Some chairs choose to vote only to avoid or break a tie. Others never vote. For the most part, however, the chair casts his or her vote at the end of the debate.

THE CHIEF EXECUTIVE

When term limits are enforced effectively, board members come and go. The chief executive, however, often stays with the organization for many years, holding the organizational memory, keeping an eye on the revolving door and often dealing with the consequences as the culture of the board shifts. Board work and meetings evolve as new members enter the scene. On most boards, the chief executive is considered as an integral participant in board meetings — ex officio or not, voting or nonvoting — and therefore is in a good position to monitor the change and use his or her influence in bringing new members up to speed and familiarizing them with the existing processes. At the same time, when established methods seem outdated and need refurbishment, it is necessary for the chief executive to listen to new ideas and implement them as is feasible.

In most nonprofits, the chief executive is not a voting member of the board — an issue that every board must discuss in order to define its own relationship with the staff leader. Voting rights, however, should not affect the role the chief executive plays at board meetings. The chief executive is an essential key figure in ensuring that the board is well equipped to make the best possible decisions and govern the organization with commitment. If this concept is actively nurtured, accepted, and embraced by individual board members, the chief executive is in an extremely powerful position to drive the organization with full backing by the board.

In reality, only a few board meetings would probably succeed or even take place if it were not for the chief executive. As the chair often takes the role of the spiritual leader and the manager of internal board member relations, the chief executive is the force behind organizing the actual meeting. She prepares the agenda and along with the chair, provides an invaluable perspective and clarity to issues on the agenda, ensures that all the logistics for the meeting are carefully executed, coordinates the production and distribution of board books, and ultimately stands behind the meeting as the organizer and a crucial participant.

BENEFITS OF KPAWN MEETINGS

One way that the board can show support for the chief executive is to install regular mini-meetings with him in an executive session, usually before every board meeting. These sessions are called KPAWN, or what Keeps the President Awake at Night meetings. For 15 minutes, allow the chief executive to talk about issues that are his biggest concerns at the moment. These topics may cover funding problems, staff retention, burnout fears, or even more personal pressures, but they all have an impact on daily work life. Divulging these important issues without fear of judgment or worry gives the leader a chance to both release some pressure in a more informal setting and discuss situations that do not necessarily belong in the official meeting agenda. The issues brought forward do not get recorded in the board meeting minutes, but it makes sense to state that the board had a private session with the chief executive. Naturally, the chief executive must use good judgment when choosing the issues that are shared with the board in order not to invite the board to micromanage or make decisions on his behalf. These sessions also allow the board members to understand and appreciate the stress factor that every nonprofit chief executive knows much too well.

Naturally, the chief executive's planning and communication with the board chair form the foundation for effective meetings. Few would deny the importance of this partnership for the overall success of the organization. In order for the partnership to be effective, these two leaders must feel comfortable with the division of labor. While both are partners in planning, the chief executive is accountable to the full board and the chair is the contact and representative of the full body.

A wise chief executive does not tell the board what to do nor does he or she have the authority to do so. The executive does the necessary homework that helps justify to the board why certain issues are critical and demand priority or overall attention. This happens by giving the board the right information in the right format, whether it is in the chief executive's report, included in the board book, or inserted into materials sent to members in between meetings. Avoiding detailed daily accounts of what happens in the office eliminates the detailed inquisition so typical of micromanaging boards. The chief executive proves to the board that its work matters when it sees that its directives have been implemented, the organization is well managed, and results are positive.

The chief executive should also remain active in suggesting and planning ways to educate board members and build their capacity. A wise executive works with the board to identify what information the board needs to provide appropriate and effective oversight.

STAFF

Very few board meetings take place without any staff present. Naturally, the chief executive is indispensable, but many of the staff members have roles to play, too. It is important to remember, however, that board meetings are business meetings for board members; they are not meetings to focus on the administrative and managerial concerns of the staff. Staff meetings exist separately for that purpose.

The staff's main role at a board meeting is to be available for consultation and to support the chief executive. While board members should respect their expertise and invite them to sit at the table, it is necessary to be clear about their respective function and clarify the reason for the invitation. If this is not done, confusion about roles may lead to staff dominating the discussion. If the chief executive has hired the right people, there is a pool of capable individuals who can give the board needed perspective on big issues that appear on the agenda: The chief financial officer knows the intricacies of the budget and the financial statements and is the best choice to answer board members' questions on those documents; the development director has the latest information on fundraising efforts as well as feedback from major funders; the program and marketing directors can clarify the gains or struggles of key program or sales efforts; and the president's report, often already included in the consent agenda, should contain highlights of the recent trends, often making it unnecessary for staff members to make additional reports unless a special focus will be placed on one of their areas of responsibility.

Staff members rarely need to sit in the room through the entire board meeting. The agenda should spell out when specific issues are being discussed and when staff members should be present. Equally, the chair or the chief executive can indicate when staff's assistance is no longer needed. If a meal is served at a meeting, staff may be invited to join the board. This allows board members to get to know senior staff — or, if feasible, the entire staff — in a more relaxed setting.

If the board has an open-door policy for all staff — as controversial as this practice may be — nonparticipating staff members do not belong around the table but should have seats at the periphery. The purpose of this policy, most likely, is to eliminate any concerns about secrecy and fears about the board making decisions that are not well-founded and debated. This practice may not be viable for most organizations as it has implications for the effective use of staff time and the meeting space may not accommodate the full staff. Also, when the board is hypothetically discussing plans that might have serious implications for staff, it might be precarious to include staff at that phase of discussion. A well-organized chief executive, under all circumstances, debriefs the staff after a board meeting. BoardSource, for example, regularly schedules a staff meeting to closely follow a board meeting. This allows the chief executive to communicate with all staff members about the board's reaction to presented issues and to explain new guidelines or directives that the board specifically articulated for the next quarter or the remainder of the year.

OUTSIDERS AND GUESTS

In addition to board members and staff, there are a variety of other people who might be present during a board meeting. What brings these individuals to the meeting depends on their possible contributions to the session, certain legal stipulations, their concern for the organization, or the overall attitude of the board that encourages outsiders. Or, looking at them from a slightly different point of view, they are either invited by the board, self-invited, or they serve a standard role during the meeting. It is important that everyone is aware of who is in the room and what each individual's role is.

Speakers and experts on specific issues under board examination are common guests of board meetings. It makes sense to bring in an outside opinion or perspective when the board is dealing with major strategic issues. Examples of these speakers might include an industry specialist who can introduce the board to field-specific questions that must be understood before setting new policy; a statistician or a pollster with data that can help open the board's eyes when new directions are being reviewed; a marketing expert to guide the board on communications issues if staff does not have this expertise. These guests often stay only for the time when their assistance is needed, or they may come as a luncheon speaker and then stay for a more informal discussion afterwards.

KEEPING HONORARY, EMERITUS, AND OTHER NONVOTING MEMBERS INFORMED

If the intention for honorary and emeritus members is to have them participate as advisors during meetings, send them invitations to the meeting along with all related materials. This would also include any regular ex officio attendee who is present due to his or her position. If your honorary members' roles have not been clarified in any manner (which should be done to avoid any confusion), do not automatically send the meeting packet. Keep honorary members informed in other ways, or only invite them to specific sessions. There is no legal obligation to send meeting materials to nonvoting members.

The board may invite a lawyer (or sometimes a parliamentarian) to join a meeting when particularly tricky issues are being handled. It is better not to engage a board member who is a lawyer for this task if the counsel ends up representing the board or the organization in a legal matter.

Equally, the board may invite an outside accountant to a meeting when specific financial issues are a concern. Naturally, there needs to be an annual meeting with the auditor. This is the board's opportunity to discuss the financial statements and the overall financial practices — internal controls, processes, policies, and staff's capacity — in an executive session without any staff present.

Many boards have nonvoting members who serve in an advisory capacity and may have an open invitation to participate in meetings. These members may be former board members or chairs, representatives from affiliates or supporting organizations, or liaisons from advisory groups.

Special meetings of the board may be organized and run by facilitators or consultants as well. Depending on their purpose, these guests may simply steer the board through a process or guide and provide input in decision making. Self-assessment, strategic planning, or preparation for a capital campaign may cause the board to engage an outside consultant.

Sometimes funders want to observe a board meeting to get a better understanding of how the board functions, what its goals are, and how it meets those goals. Or, funders may be invited to attend to see how the board demonstrates a readiness in undertaking a new endeavor or to continue the present course that may be specifically dear to that funder.

Constituents may demand an opportunity to deliver a communiqué to the board. If the chair and the chief executive have assessed that a formal board meeting is the right place and method to inform the board (rather than handling the issue outside of the boardroom), it may be a good opportunity to keep the board abreast of the constituent issues. Some constituents may have a desire and could benefit from having a chance to monitor closely the organization's governance processes and decisions.

Other customers and clients may also be asked to come and give a testimony of how they have benefited from the organization. These testimonies can have a powerful effect on the motivation of board members, and the board meeting is a perfect venue for encouraging the full board as a group.

Boards functioning under sunshine laws do not have the luxury to plan outsiders' attendance. If the meetings are open to the public, anyone interested may be in the room. As discussed in Chapter 1, it is acceptable and desirable to communicate behavioral rules and process details to observers. Experience may gradually train the meeting organizers to anticipate the size of the observing crowd or, when particularly controversial or otherwise tricky issues are on the published agenda, prepare for vocal guests.

If the board does not have to follow sunshine laws, outsiders should be admitted by invitation only. When issues discussed in the boardroom are not yet ready for public discussion or otherwise need to be handled confidentially, the board can always retreat to an executive session if the situation so requires. Logistically, it is helpful for the staff to know how many people are going to be present and what other arrangements may be needed. Without a policy or a procedure for inviting guests, under some circumstances, either divisive or negligent board members may willingly or accidentally create situations that are difficult to manage or that cause undue stress for staff.

It is not uncommon to find boards that openly invite outsiders to their meetings. These boards consider transparency as a priority and have a need to send a message that there are absolutely no secrets within the organization and its leaders. When this message is communicated, guests tend to appreciate the opportunity to observe the board in action.

ORGANIZATIONAL MEMBERS

Membership organizations should have a clear understanding of state laws as they pertain to their members' legal access to documents, financial data, and board meetings. Many state statutes provide members of a nonprofit with the explicit right to inspect minutes and other books and records. Confidential donor information is not included. However, inspection must be for proper purposes, in good faith, and not for feeding individual curiosity or for blackmail purposes.

Whether members have easy access to the boardroom or not, it is imperative for members to understand their relationship to the board. In many cases, the membership elects the board. Membership organizations serve the members who as such have considerable power to approve major organizational decisions. The board may be obligated to seek membership approval on major resolutions. This does not mean that members have the right to second-guess every board decision or have a say in all aspects of governance. By electing the right board members, organizational members have already exercised their right to influence the organization's internal affairs.

BOARD MEMBER CANDIDATES

Inviting board member candidates to attend board meetings may not be the best way for the governance committee, or the rest of the board, to determine whether he or she is a good prospect. But it can certainly give the candidates one more opportunity to judge whether the board might be a good fit for them. By observing the board in action — even in a fleeting action — the candidates have a better chance to determine how efficient and focused it is; and to get a good sense of the atmosphere in the boardroom. These observations can influence the prospects' opinions to either accept the invitation or to stay as far away from the board as possible!

REMEMBER

- Each person in the boardroom has a purpose — whether that person votes or not. Make sure all participants understand why they are there or allowed or invited to be there.

- As the chief executive, provide relevant background information that forms the basis of discussion.

- Naturally, no meeting takes place without board members. Attend every meeting: This is your opportunity to shape the future of the organization.

- Invite outsiders to provide additional expertise or scrutiny.

CASE STUDY
HEAL THYSELF

The board of the GHI Free Clinic had set aside time at the end of its meeting for a celebration in honor of reaching a difficult goal. The 27-member board had finally achieved balance and diversity. It now had equal representation of its three primary "constituent" groups: doctors, pharmaceutical company executives, and low-income users of the clinic's services. It had taken the board more than a year to identify and recruit its new members, and today's meeting was the first one attended by all members of all three groups.

Halfway through the meeting, Daryl, the board chair, noticed that all of the doctors were sitting at one end of the table and the pharmaceutical executives were clustered together at the other end. And he hadn't heard a single word from any of the low-income clients.

If things continued this way, the board would have achieved diversity in name only, and it wouldn't have much of substance to celebrate. How, Daryl wondered, had they not anticipated a situation like this and taken steps to avoid it? Was there anything he could do now to change the dynamics in the room and salvage the meeting?

Diversity for the sake of diversity does not automatically add value. When issues of power and comfort come into play, feelings of uneasiness commonly lead to clustering in like groups or posturing to show value while leaving others out. What breaks this pattern is leadership that focuses on creating a board that leverages its diversity and builds a culture where everyone feels included.

Fortunately, the meeting can be salvaged. Daryl should thank everyone who has been actively engaged in the discussions and then announce a five-minute break. Thanking board members for their thoughtful comments and insight reinforces that active participation is welcomed and encouraged.

When the meeting reconvenes, Daryl should ask board members to take a seat next to someone they do not know in an effort to get the group out of its "comfort zone" and to help broaden the conversation. As an example, he himself should move next to someone new.

If the conversation continues to be dominated by the doctors and executives, then Daryl might ask the board what perspectives are missing from the conversation. Sometimes a pointed question like this will help the conversation "dominators" realize that not everyone around the table is participating in the discussions. After the meeting, Daryl should approach the quiet members and encourage them to speak up.

Going forward, the board should provide the members with opportunities to get to know each other informally and add training or coaching on building diverse teams to the board development plan.

Adapted from the May/June 2007 (Volume 16, Number 3) edition of *Board Member®*.

CHAPTER 6

OVERCOMING CULTURAL AND BEHAVIORAL BARRIERS

Q Our board meetings lost their vitality after a new member (with legal background) joined the board. He questions every issue, every process, every decision. He has such a semantic approach to everything that it seems we are simply turning in circles and not going forward with our business. As the chair, what can I do to get back to our old ways?

A It seems that the culture of your board meetings has changed since the new member arrived. You have an engaged member but his focus seems to be more on process rather than on results. He wants to ensure that legally you are doing everything correctly. That is not a bad thing in itself but, he has managed to take the board as a prisoner of the process. As the chair, you have the reins to fix the situation.

- Take the board member aside and get to know what his concerns are to understand his approach to board meetings.

- If he has specific examples that are valid concerns about your board decisions or process, explain to him the whats and whys. And if necessary, fix the issues.

- Take charge of the board meetings. If a board member wants to rehash an issue that is already decided, explain succinctly that this is no longer necessary. Handle the more detailed explanations after the meeting.

- Suggest that this board member take an assignment to assess your board processes and provide suggestions for improvement. Remind him that you are not in a courtroom — you need to follow appropriate steps but a solid and open exchange of opinions is part of arriving at good decisions. Deliberation benefits from absence of strict parliamentary order.

- Have the full board address his recommendations and make a full board decision to agree on your meeting culture. As the "elephant in the room" is liberated, it will be easier to get back into business.

- And always question whether the "old ways" are the right ways and worthy of bringing back.

Board members have a surprisingly demanding and varied job to do. Rarely can one board member fulfill most of the board's necessary functions. If that were the case, few boards would need more than two or three members, board meetings would simply serve as the venues to confirm assumptions and record expected decisions, and this small group would never realize what it is missing and not accomplishing.

Various backgrounds and experiences (professional and personal, as well as cultural and ethical) add to the quality of the board. Other important characteristics can include leadership skills, community involvement, public recognition, political connections, fundraising capacities, and shared values and commitment. Familiarity with the organization's field and issues can be important. Sometimes the presence of a few donors, professional insiders, customers, and clients can positively benefit the organization. These examples all focus on maximizing the special value of each board member in the organization.

How your board members carry out their duties, communicate with each other, work as a team, or solve problems are all very important factors in defining the culture of your board. These factors can result in an efficient and productive team that works well together. They also can do the opposite, if your focus is on the external aspects of your group's working methods and not on the core purpose of its meetings. Only by looking at your processes in more detail can you determine whether you have a group hung up on processes, or one that is continuously accomplishing something important. Finding new board members who easily fit within your culture — or bringing in members who see a need to change this atmosphere — can be an option in your recruitment efforts. However, your chair ultimately has the best chance to influence the culture, habits, or the "ethos" of your board and its interactions.

A good board is made up of a diverse group of people with varying skills, expertise, and modes of operation. Deliberation benefits from this diversity but, let's face it, communication is not simple when unique personalities try to get their message across! People can be either extroverts or introverts, articulate or tongue-tied, passionate or unconcerned, altruistic or selfish. Board members are there for different reasons and possess differing attributes. Some may be there to learn more, while others may want to teach others. Some focus on the little details and others see the big picture. Some are team players, and others highly individualistic. Unfortunately, some may have private agendas and are self-absorbed. All of these qualities and characteristics — and many others — must work together, or the board will spend an inordinate time solving communication problems and unnecessary misunderstandings.

As we discussed in Chapter 4, every board needs some structure for its internal operations. Without it, you do not have a common reference to rely on when the unexpected happens. Specific standards serve as a guide to do the right thing and help you solve dilemmas that arise from individual board member behavior. At the other end of the spectrum, too much structure and too many rules can stifle creativity and make the board focus more on rules than results. Understanding the legal and ethical expectations placed on boards and being familiar with topics that drive group dynamics are good starting points for defining the effectiveness of your board. That knowledge is also what you want to find in new recruits.

How do your board members communicate with each other? Is there a general respect of differing opinions? Can you all disagree respectfully? In fact, do you encourage differing opinions and challenging points of view? If you answer yes, you probably have a board that is open to new ways of doing things and that does not form cliques that fight with each other.

If your organization serves a community in flux, provides services to a multitude of cultural and ethnic constituents, or wants to reach out to new groups of potential customers and clients, probably nothing is as important as striving for ethnic diversity on your board. Your leadership sends the message to staff and to the outside world that diversity and inclusiveness are valued. If understanding the issues of your constituents is important to be able to meet their needs, your board must set the tone and show how organizational decisions reflect and respond to this need. To facilitate this decision-making challenge in a group of individuals with differing backgrounds, try some of following practices:

- Avoid tokenism. Commit to diversity, and don't expect your board members to fill a quota. No individual should or can represent a specific segment of a society. If you do not give your members a label, you have a better chance to concentrate on the content and skill they bring to your decisions.

- Treat each board member equally. Share board responsibilities according to interest and capacity. Expect everyone to contribute to discussion and value everybody's point of view.

- Cultivate acceptance toward differing opinions. Seeking agreement on the broadest issues first creates a strong foundation for debate. The role of the chair as a mediator cannot be overestimated. At the end of the debate, however, it is important that each board member respects the democratic process and is able to represent the official position to the outside world.

- Provide cross-cultural training. Understanding how different cultures make decisions and handle conflict can play a big role in facilitating communication.

- Allow time for board members to get to know each other. Making time for the members to socialize and communicate with each other outside of a meeting fosters the camaraderie necessary for teamwork.

EMPOWER YOUTH

Electing young people to the board might be the wisest decision some organizations ever make. If your organization deals with youth issues, including the youth perspective in your discussions seems to be common sense. If state laws do not forbid minors from serving on your board, it still is important to take some precautions to protect everyone from any potential liabilities. Consider the following points:

- Clarify in your organizational documents that you intend to engage young people on your board.

- Understand all the risks and obstacles that you may encounter.

- Include a clause in your bylaws allowing you to elect young people as board members.

- Do not elect young people as officers or other leadership positions where they might have to sign contracts or other official documents.

- Use committees and other task forces to provide additional leadership and training opportunities for young people.

- Realize the additional flexibility needed to organize your board meetings around commuting to meetings, school schedules, generational communication challenges, and inexperience with certain financial aspects of the board member role.

KEEPING CIVILITY IN THE BOARDROOM

Sometimes, board members let their emotions override objectivity. Passion, in and of itself, is not a bad thing. It often reflects the deep commitment and concern that a board member has for the organization's mission and work. Particularly, when the organization works with children, animals, the environment, and other social issues, some board members tend to fight for their specific beliefs in the boardroom. When emotional reactions are directed at fellow members in a negative manner, private wrangling can divert the focus from what the board is supposed to be doing.

Civility in the boardroom indicates that board members understand and accept the idea that differing opinions are to be treasured, welcomed, and encouraged. Members need to know how to listen and let their peers express their opinions, no matter how esoteric or impossible they may seem, and to respect each other's points of view. Certainly debates can become heated, especially when an issue is controversial, delicate, contentious, troublesome, or touchy. The chair should be careful to look for the signs that the discussion may be getting out of hand and take measures to keep the situation under control.

Few boards have escaped disorderly meetings. If a board member dominates discussion and seems to have all the answers, the chair must find a moment to intercept and turn the faucet off. Some boards may need to follow a more structured process in this case and respect a certain level of parliamentary order. This makes it easier for the chair to control the floor and grant individual members the opportunity to take their turn.

Q **Last year, we recruited a community leader as a board member. She has been a generous donor in the past, so it seemed like she would be a good fit. However, it soon became evident that her strong religious beliefs do not fully match the open culture we have enjoyed in our board. She is very assertive and moralizing during meetings, and many members resent her, though no one dares to say anything. Is there a way to restrain her or is this a lost cause?**

A Where is your chair? Have your fellow board members discussed with her their uneasiness or irritation with the religious overtone your meetings have taken? It is natural to feel uncomfortable about contradicting a person who expresses her strong faith but there is a place for religious manifestation, and it is not necessarily in the boardroom. If your organization is not there to proselytize a certain religious practice, then it is not necessarily appropriate to allow that to dominate your board meetings.

Your chair should take the person aside and explain nicely but firmly the effect her words have on others. The chair could use herself as an example and explain that many of the comments seem demeaning to her and have the same effect on several others. If your board is like most, you have members with different approaches to faith issues, which they keep to themselves during the meetings. This board member may change her inappropriate behavior if you simply make her aware of it. If not, then perhaps she should serve another organization.

In the future, assess your recruitment methods to include a review of previous board performance. Don't be dazzled by generous annual checks.

If a board member uses improper language, verbally insults or ridicules fellow members, or otherwise attacks someone personally, the situation should be stopped right away. If immediate change does not occur, and the member does not apologize for the language or the comment, he or she should be asked to leave the room. Disagreeing with someone's comments or arguments is perfectly normal, but inappropriate personal behavior in a professional setting should not be accepted. If abusive and misdirected behavior continues, the board may want to consider removing the offending member from the board.

Racist and other ethnic comments, intolerance of other members' personal convictions, and impugning the motives of others should all be considered unacceptable in the boardroom. Whether the comments are intentional or out of ignorance, they deserve immediate attention. After clarifying the problem with the board member, the chair should then consider whether some diversity training is in order for the board.

If a board member has a personal problem relating to excessive alcohol or other substance abuse, and it spills over negatively to his or her board service, the chair or another trusted peer should discuss the issue privately with the member.

Whether dire behaviors are unintentional or deliberate, they divert the board's attention and energies in the wrong direction, and waste valuable time. Boards with problematic members may be able to learn some helpful tips and solutions for dealing with their problems by speaking with members from other boards.

Q **Our organization has programs in other countries and our board has made special efforts to recruit members from those areas. The intention has been noble but we truly struggle with cultural differences. How can we address these differences without further frustration?**

A You are trying to break barriers, and that is admirable. A culturally diverse board means finding different ways to communicate, and the effort is on everyone's shoulders. Here are some ideas:

- Select an official language for the board. If the board chooses to have multiple languages, make sure that competent translators are available.

- Adopt a common language glossary. Make it free of jargon, and provide an explanation of commonly used terms in a nonprofit board setting.

- Create standards for written and presentation materials. Consistent formats and terminology may help non–native speakers quickly understand the material presented.

- Provide cross-cultural training. Understanding how different cultures make decisions and handle conflict can play a big role in facilitating communication.

- Send out the agenda well in advance of the meeting. Because mailing items to a foreign country typically takes longer than mailing to a U.S. address, considering sending board materials electronically so that board members have time to study the materials and prepare questions before the meeting. This is especially helpful if your board uses consent agendas, where the board votes on a block of items without discussing them in the meeting.

- Be clear about expectations of board members. New members with roots in non-U.S. contexts may have radically different assumptions about what it means to serve on the board of a nonprofit organization. Careful orientation is a must.

- Allow time for board members to get to know each other. Making time for the members to socialize and communicate with each other outside of a meeting fosters the camaraderie necessary for teamwork.

MANAGING CONFLICTS OF INTEREST

The affiliations, interests, and business relationships of active board members may also impact the decisions and transactions of the boards on which they serve. This can be particularly true if there is an overlap between the issues a member deals with in his or her private life and those the board is addressing. This is a fairly common situation and the key is how the board manages the conflict.

Uninfluenced and independent decision making is of primary importance for every board member. Private objectives, personal benefit, or private inurement should not be the driving force when members of the board discuss the internal business of the organization. Board members must rely on their own conscience when deciding what the best action is for the organization; thus bringing back the concept of duty of loyalty, which is one of the legal obligations that individual board members must embrace. When serving on a board, a member's loyalties should first lie with the organization's mission and constituency.

When faced with a conflict of interest, the board's only safe harbor is addressing the issue effectively and directly. If the board already has a conflict-of-interest policy, take time to re-evaluate its contents:

- Is it clear what constitutes a conflict of interest?

- Who is affected by the policy?

- Who are disqualified individuals on the board and staff?

- What are the steps to eliminating a conflict of interest when the board discusses and votes on issues?

- Whose role is it to enforce the policy?

If the policy clearly states that a board member with a conflict of interest is not allowed to vote or participate in the discussion and will be asked to leave the room, the board is obligated to enforce the policy. This is how a board shows accountability and is able to prove that its decision-making process is intact.

Asking board members to sign a disclosure form at the beginning of each year helps to create an atmosphere of openness. The purpose of the form is to have each board member list possible points of conflict during the coming year. The list should include financial, business, and personal affiliations that might somehow affect the board member's capacity to make untainted judgments. Naturally, it is impossible to predict what issues might affect the impartiality of any board member ahead of time. Each case is situation specific, and every potential conflict of interest must be addressed on a case-by-case basis. By creating a preliminary list of conflicts, the chair can keep an eye on eventual sticky points. If new conflicts arise during the year, it is expected that a board member in question step forward and recuse him- or herself in accordance with the policy.

If a board member "forgets" to bring up a conflict-of-interest issue during a board meeting, it is up to the chair to address it. Likewise, if someone else on the board is aware of the conflict, but the chair is not, it is up to the individual to share the information with the chair. Some tact is necessary. If there is a disagreement on the facts or how the conflict presents itself, the executive committee or the full board can be asked to make the ultimate decision.

BRINGING PRIVATE AGENDAS INTO THE BOARDROOM

Private agendas may inhibit some board members from demonstrating their undivided loyalty to the organization. What is a private agenda? A private agenda is personal interests, preferences, or goals that divert the focus of a board member from the organizational issue to that of a private matter. For instance: A board member proposes the creation of a program that benefits his or her child; a board member lobbies for the recruitment of a new member who backs his or her vision for a future direction or action; or a member has aspirations for a leadership role and gradually manages to manipulate and create an inner clique in favor of his or her platform.

In fact, a private agenda is pure conflict of interest and may hover close to private inurement or private benefit. Private agendas do not belong in the boardroom, and it is the responsibility of fellow board members to bring the issue to the attention of the chair if the chair is not aware of it. It is the chair's job to remind all members of their duty of care and loyalty to the mission and to the organization. These duties can be respected only by objective and unbiased decision making.

CULTURE OF INQUIRY

To be able to get to the heart of the matter at the boardroom table, members of the board must be willing to listen to, share, accept, and respect comments and opinions presented by fellow members. Everyone should have an opportunity to express his or her opinion and, at the same time, should expect that these opinions may be further explored. These attitudes demonstrate key characteristics of a true culture of inquiry.

Within a culture of inquiry, board members have a presence of mind to make a decision that drives from the obligation and need to help the organization. Board members rely on candor and thorough reflection, ask questions until all sides of an issue have been aired, dare to contradict or question present practices or traditions, and are not influenced by seniority, position, or reputation of a fellow board or staff member or a donor. In short, a thorough deliberation allows a board member to learn all the facets of an issue and then to distill their peers' perspectives into an autonomous and educated opinion.

ELECTING A DEVIL'S ADVOCATE AND DEVIL'S INQUISITOR

To push a board into thinking more creatively or to unblock tendencies of stagnation, the board may want to create an official position of a "devil's advocate." By choosing a single member, or rotating the job among board members, the devil's advocate has the role of purposefully contradicting presented arguments. As long as it is understood that this is the intended role of the board member during the meeting, the board can turn the idea into a productive game. The "devil's advocate du jour" will not feel left out of the actual debate if he simply makes sure his point of view comes up during the discussion or as one of the counterpoints or questions.

You may also encourage board members to serve as "devil's inquisitors." The role of these individuals is not to purposefully contradict a statement or position but to always ask the questions that nobody else wants to ask, those difficult questions that one normally finds embarrassing or "dumb." The purpose of these questions is to clarify and simplify the issue under discussion and to ensure that everyone ultimately is on the same page and has at least a basic understanding of the details. These questions can come in handy particularly when the board is looking at the financial statements, and everyone is not a financial wizard.

No argument should be off limits as long as it does not get personal and it encourages members to consider alternative options. Any exercise that forces a board to open up to new ideas can turn an ordinary board into a vigorous and insightful group of team members. However, a perennial devil's advocate or inquisitor may eventually test the board's patience, at which time the game becomes counterproductive.

Q We have an exceptionally diverse — and exceptionally challenging — board. How can we build more cohesion and agreement into our decision making and avoid constant split votes?

A Diversity among board members often means that numerous points of view need to learn to live together. Deliberate disconnection often originates from personality clashes and differences in personal aspirations or ambitions. These expressions are symptoms of deeper problems on the board. This kind of a divide needs particular attention and must be solved or the board will need a referee at each meeting. Try the following suggestions to work out a solution.

- Use committees and task forces to prepare the board for discussion on controversial issues.

- Assign task force leadership positions for your most vocal members.

- Send out committee materials and other support material in board books and expect board members to have read them.

- Agree on objectives before starting the discussion to eliminate a possible preliminary stumbling block.

- Test different decision-making processes outlined earlier in this book.

- If time allows, table the issue, do more research, and come back to the next meeting with fresh ideas.

- Rely on the chair's final judgment if he or she votes to break a tie.

REMEMBER

- Seek different habits, backgrounds, traditions, experiences, and skills to open the collective board's eyes and avoid stagnation. Remember that diversity on a board does not necessarily make communication and interaction between its members easier.

- Never allow private agendas and conflicts of interest to drive a member's motivations.

CASE STUDY
PERSISTENT AND PERSNICKETY

Although Evelyn was very bright, attended every board meeting, was always well prepared, and truly cared about the LMN Organization, she was driving the board nuts! It was Evelyn-fatigued.

Because of the nature of the organization, the board had to review and make policy decisions on a frequent basis. Every time an issue came up, Evelyn insisted on discussing it to death. As a result, meetings took twice as long as they should. Then, if the board reached a decision that Evelyn didn't agree with, she continued to fight it by mentioning it again and again at future meetings and voicing her opinion offline. Her colleagues on the board were very polite and tried to be respectful, but enough was enough!

When a board member refuses to bow to majority decision, it causes high frustration among the group, wastes time and energy, and ultimately lowers the value of the individual's contributions because the other board members will consider him or her an obstacle to the team. Once a full discussion has happened, a vote has been taken, and a majority opinion has been made, it is imperative that all board members support that decision both publicly and privately.

The board chair of the LMN Organization should consider taking the following actions:

- Broach the subject in private with Evelyn, thanking her for her contributions but asking her to support all decisions once they have been voted on.

- If the behavior continues, adopt a strategy in the public forum, such as the one illustrated in the following scenario:

Evelyn: "Madam Chairman, I would like to bring up the policy we voted on last week. As you know, I am on the record as opposing this policy and really think we need to revisit it. For example, I've been thinking about…"

Board chair: "Excuse me, Evelyn. I want to thank you for your continued concern about this issue. We have explored this issue extensively and are now on record with a decision. The vote last week was 9–1 against. It will only be reopened for discussion upon the receipt in writing of significant factual data that warrant such."

Handled in this direct manner, it will be made clear to Evelyn that unless she has additional support from other board members or strong evidence that a decision was made without the appropriate information at hand, matters once discussed and voted upon will be closed once and for all. If a board member does not support a decision for whatever reason, he or she must remain silent or step down from the board.

Adapted from *Taming the Troublesome Board Member* by Katha Kissman, BoardSource, 2006.

CHAPTER 7
OTHER KINDS OF MEETINGS

Q A board I just joined successfully engages all members in different committees. The committees always meet just before the board meeting, as it is the most cost-effective way to bring committee members together. Our board meetings end up serving as show-and-tell sessions for the committee chairs. What could I suggest to change this "bad" habit?

A This approach does not recognize the variety of roles committees play. It tends to fit all committees in the same mold, regardless of their task. Some committees are action oriented and do not fit in a predetermined mold; they need flexibility. Some committees can address their issues in an hour, others may need half a day. Also, this approach does not allow the committee chairs to carefully prepare a report for the board but expects them to do, as you say, a show-and-tell immediately afterwards. How about including an item in your next board meeting "How Can We Best Benefit from the Work of Our Committees?" and discuss alternate approaches altogether. Here are some suggestions:

- Ask committee chairs to take the lead and define the modus operandi for their meetings.

- Conference calls or other electronic communication methods work wonders for some committees. Physical presence may not even be necessary.

- Consider grouping committee members by location. Those living close to each other may find it easier to come to meetings.

- Insist on written reports for all committees that will be included in your consent agenda.

This book would be incomplete without a discussion of the meetings board members are required to attend outside of the traditional board meeting. Meetings are simply a part of the way board work gets accomplished. Whether it is the very first meeting of the board, the board's annual meeting, or regular committee meetings, this chapter defines the purposes for these other kinds of meetings. Also included in this chapter is a discussion of membership meetings, the role of the executive committee in special sessions, and the value of holding executive sessions.

FIRST MEETING OF THE FOUNDING BOARD

There is a first for everything, including board meetings. In fact, the first board meeting is of great importance as it brings the board together officially for the first time and sets the tone for future meetings. The founder(s) may have brought potential board members together several times before — individually or as a group — but the first official meeting is the founding meeting of the organization. Any previous get-togethers most likely have been informal gatherings or communications to kick off the planning period or to become better acquainted socially.

During the first meeting, the board will need to approve the purpose of the organization. It has a task to elect officers and grant them needed authority to act on behalf of the organization. This may include the right to sign checks and organizational documents, open bank accounts, or represent the board or the organization when necessary. If the bylaws have not yet been written, this meeting should start the process. The board should assign the job of creating the first draft of the bylaws to an individual or a task force. Another committee or a task force can accomplish all other necessary procedures relating to the formation of the nonprofit. Depending on the type of nonprofit the group is creating, additional task forces may be formed to research and acquire the necessary licenses, permissions, and insurance policies; search for office space and purchase office furniture and equipment; draft brochures and other documents; and detail immediate program plans and service strategies.

To immediately get the board started on the right foot, a conscientious founder makes sure that proper governance procedures receive appropriate attention. If members of the founding board are unfamiliar with the roles and responsibilities of board service, it is crucial to set aside the time to study good practices for effective boards. Every board member should have an orientation to board service, liability issues, and roles and responsibilities of individual board members and boards as a collective group. Ensuring that recruitment of future board members is set in motion right from the start is simply smart planning. If outside experts are needed for these tasks, arrange for the board to meet with them. Forming a capable and responsible board from the beginning helps to secure the future of the organization and sets proper risk management processes in motion.

Prior to or at the beginning of the first meeting, identify who will be taking the meeting minutes. Besides divvying up the tasks during the first meeting, the board will need to set up a schedule for future meetings. Before the next full board meeting takes place, the minutes of the first meeting need to be ready for approval. These minutes will serve as the reference for the foundation of the board of this new nonprofit organization.

ANNUAL MEETING

Surprisingly, there seems to be considerable confusion about the necessity and purpose of annual meetings. An annual meeting refers to a meeting that every board of a nonprofit corporation must convene once a year in order to fill vacancies on the board, elect officers, and to approve any necessary actions to keep the organization and the board functioning. Unlike other meetings held throughout the year, the annual meeting is required by law. Most state laws indicate that an annual meeting is necessary. Naturally this does not mean that one meeting is enough for the board to carry out its duties but, as we stated previously, laws speak in *de minimis* language.

In practical terms, an annual meeting forces the board to tend to necessary business on a regular basis. It does not mean that all compulsory issues must be squeezed into an annual meeting, but that all compulsory issues need attention. If this does not happen in one meeting, there must be additional meetings throughout the year.

If there are no vacancies, naturally no elections take place. However, sharing annual reports and financial statements and approving a budget are other activities that the board must attend to. This item sharing and approval can take place during the annual meeting — as can any other usual business that requires attention.

Unless state law specifically stipulates when the annual meeting should take place, most annual meetings occur at the very beginning of the fiscal year. For example, if the fiscal year ends in December, it is common to have the annual meeting in January. This facilitates the tracking of terms for board members, allows the board to start the year with a new budget, and provides time for the chief executive to reflect on the past year's accomplishments.

See page 98 for additional discussion on annual meetings relating to membership organizations.

SPECIAL OR EMERGENCY MEETINGS: TAKING CARE OF THE UNFORESEEN

No matter how well the board predicts the future, foresees possible problems, or has a sense for otherwise unpredictable events, it must be prepared for a potential need for emergency or special meetings. On top of regularly scheduled meetings, there should be provisions for calling special meetings, the guidelines for which should be spelled out in the bylaws.

If suddenly the chief executive can no longer carry out the duty of managing the organization, a scandal revealed in the daily paper surprises a board member, or if there is a sudden change in the financial status of the organization, an emergency meeting most likely becomes necessary. Any situation that requires the immediate attention of the board can warrant a special session. Other special meetings may not have a catastrophic undertone but still require the board to react before the next regular meeting. These situations may address serious constituents' complaints, time-sensitive approval of financial transactions, or handling of opportunities that would be missed if the board waited any longer.

The bylaws should indicate how to define a special meeting, who can call one to order, how much notice is required, how many board members need to be present, and how to share the decision with those board members who were not able to attend. It is important to eliminate the use of special meetings for deviant purposes — to use them in a manipulative manner to enforce decisions that would be difficult to obtain under normal circumstances. Some boards have executive committees empowered to take first action under emergency circumstances. Please see page 95 for more information on executive committee meetings.

COMMITTEE MEETINGS: THE BOARD'S WORKSHOP

There is hardly a board member who has not attended a committee or a task force meeting. In fact, most board work is accomplished through committees. Committees and task forces do the legwork for the board or digest comprehensive materials into a manageable format. (For a more complete discussion on committees and how they work, see *The Committee Series,* referenced in the Suggested Resources section.) Committees come in all shapes and sizes; this influences the manner in which meetings are conducted. Communication differs whether there are three people in the room or 20. The more committee members, the more structure is needed in order to avoid possible chaos.

A committee is generally part of the overall board structure, has a specific charge, and may be stipulated in the bylaws, e.g., governance committee, executive committee, and financial committees. A task force is organized to research a particular issue for later recommendation and debate by the board, or carry out a specific objective within a certain amount of time. Task forces are established on an as-needed basis, as opposed to standing committees, and allow for greater flexibility in the work of the board and its structure. Members of an action committee, a committee that is primarily involved in the actual work of the organization (setting up special events, lobbying, making field visits), may not work in a meeting room at all but rather find themselves carrying out specific tasks in the field.

Committee leadership sets the tone of the meeting and an experienced facilitator can help produce positive results. The level of formality is often influenced by the preference of a committee chair. As there are no legal guidelines to determine how a committee must function, the leadership impacts the processes, involvement of members, and overall effectiveness of the group. Some meetings follow a strict order; others resemble more of a social gathering. The governance committee can undertake training for committee chairs as deemed necessary as an additional step in the board's overall leadership development.

Whether a committee keeps minutes or not is up to the group to decide. Like any group assigned with a task, it makes sense to take notes. These notes may resemble standard minutes or they may be organized in any other coherent manner. As long as they serve the purpose of recording important group decisions and communicating the accomplishments of the session, they add value.

The minutes of a committee meeting are not the same as the committee report prepared for board review. The full board does not need to know how the committee meeting was structured but, rather, what the committee suggests for board action, what information the board must have at its disposal before it can proceed, and what other information is relevant for collective decision making. The report should follow a format that eliminates unnecessary details and leaves behind a well-digested and comprehensive account of what the committee accomplished. If this issue is not clear to committee chairs, the board chair or the governance committee should ensure that proper education takes place.

Q **At our committee meeting there were two members who disagreed with the final committee recommendation for the board. What should these two members do when the board discusses the recommendation: state their disagreement, bring up new options that already were discussed in the committee, or keep quiet during the discussion?**

A The role these two committee members play depends partially on the importance of the issue, but, to preserve integrity of the board process, they should stand by the committee decision and not actively advocate against it. It might be a good idea for the committee to have a SOP (Standing Operating Procedure) for board recommendations.

- State the issue under discussion.

- Indicate that multiple options were considered.

- If you address a "standard" issue, offer the committee recommendation with its strengths and weaknesses. Indicate that the decision was not unanimous.

- If you address a "major" issue, the committee may offer the board multiple options with their strengths and downsides and how to resolve them.

- If the committee arrived at a unanimous recommendation, present it as is.

- If you are dealing with a major controversy, the committee's role is to do the leg work for the board and frame the issue adequately for full board discussion.

The committee has the obligation to bring its best thinking to the board. At the same time, the board should not serve as a rubber stamp and it has the right to ask questions and discuss the issue.

Committees are charged with bringing recommendations to the board and cannot make organizational decisions, no matter how profound their conclusions. Under normal circumstances the board is not obligated to follow the committee's suggestions. It hopefully is able to assess the committee reports' validity and totality and, after that, proceed to make a final decision. A competent committee may have non–board members as expert advisors as well as board members in training who may provide out-of-the-ordinary questions and perspectives during discussion.

Equally, even if committee or task force members do not bear the same liability for their decisions as full-fledged board members, they are bound by the same ethical and moral standards. It is wise to ensure that committee volunteers are covered by the same directors' and officers' liability insurance that protects board members.

HOW DO BOARD MEETINGS DIFFER FROM COMMITTEE MEETINGS?

Issue	Board Meetings	Committee Meetings
Purpose	Make organizational and board-specific decisions	Draft recommendations for board action and carry out tasks assigned by the board
Composition	Elected board members (with a vote); advisors (nonvoting members)	Board members; former board members; outside experts or organizational members; volunteers
Frequency	Determined by need; legally must have an annual meeting; special meetings possible	Determined by scope and purpose of task
Accountability	Board works for the organization	Committees work for the board
Attendance	Required (duty of care)	Volunteer commitment to share work load
Liability	Decisions are legally binding; personal liability if members are not meeting duties of care and loyalty	Decisions are only recommendations; normally no collective or personal liability
Structure	Some parliamentary order is necessary; bylaws and policies define details	Determined by the committee chair
Reporting	Minutes are a legal document	Reporting is informational; no legal obligation exists

EXECUTIVE COMMITTEE MEETINGS

Forming an executive committee is not necessarily a standard board resolution. Many boards manage to function perfectly efficiently without one. If a board determines that an executive committee could be structurally and functionally helpful, the committee's role and limit of authority must be defined in the bylaws.

A carefully designed executive committee may serve different purposes, which in turn will determine the structure of its meetings.

- Acting on behalf of the board: The traditional role of the executive committee is to make decisions when it is not possible or necessary to convene the full board. It is the only standing committee that, when it meets, may act as a mini-board, even if the full board should confirm the decision during the next board meeting. Under emergency conditions, the meetings may bring the committee members together without much preparation, or the meeting may take place over the phone and compel the members to use their best judgment without much background information.

- Sounding board: If the role of the committee is to provide overall support for the chief executive, the meetings may be carried on over the telephone. Burning issues determine the agenda.

- Strategic coordinator: If the executive committee is the master coordinator of board work, the committee will likely meet regularly and work as the board's complexity mandates. If its task is to guide the board's focus, its meetings should be closely synchronized with board meetings. This type of executive committee works on the organization's priorities and strategic items and ensures that board meetings will not linger on administrative matters.

- Evaluator: If the executive committee's duty is to administer the performance evaluation of the chief executive, it should do exactly that, meeting with the full board afterwards to deliver the final assessment results.

Because of the variety of responsibilities that can be delegated to an executive committee, it is often impossible to plan a schedule ahead of time or anticipate when the committee should meet. This is a demand that executive committee members need to understand and accept.

In order to prevent the appearance of the executive committee as an exclusive "inner circle," the executive committee should always keep meeting minutes. If the committee makes decisions for the board, it must be able to document the circumstances of these decisions. The minutes must be distributed to every board member after the meeting. If the meeting consists of chatting with the chief executive, official minutes clearly are not necessary, but notes are. Notes serve as a record of the conversation and as a reminder of specific recommendations or points that need attention.

MAKING USE OF EXECUTIVE SESSIONS

An executive committee meeting and an executive session are not synonymous. As previously described, an executive committee is a standing committee of the board; an executive session is an exclusive meeting behind closed doors where the purpose determines who is present. Besides some executive committee meetings, if there is one meeting that tends to create anxiety, suspicion, and sense of secrecy, it is an executive session.

All boards have the right to meet without outsiders in the room. There are situations when the presence of staff, including the chief executive, or other nonmembers may hinder open deliberation. Some situations demand confidentiality and must be handled in privacy. Other circumstances simply allow board members to have a moment to share feelings and opinions about their respective relationships and their role vis-à-vis the organization. But the board can also meet in an executive session with the chief executive. KPAWN meetings are described on page 70.

WHEN IS AN EXECUTIVE SESSION NECESSARY?

The following circumstances may demand confidentiality, candid exchange of opinions, or protection of individual rights:

- Investigation of alleged improper conduct by a board member

- Discussion of financial issues with an auditor

- Preparation for a case with a lawyer

- Exploration of planning for major endeavors, such as mergers or real estate deals

- Discussion of the board's approach to a scandal or negative publicity

- Handling of personnel issues, such as chief executive compensation, performance evaluation, or disciplinary issues

- Handling of any other matters where confidentiality has been requested or is otherwise prudent

- Peer-to-peer discussions about board operations

There are also clear rules when an executive session is not in order. Boards should not revert to executive sessions for any of the following reasons: to avoid discussing tough issues in the open; to dodge responsibility; to restrict any board member's access to information by excluding him or her from a meeting; to purposefully create a secret society atmosphere and air of suspicion. The purpose of the session must be clear ahead of time and as soon as the issue has been handled, a regular meeting should proceed. The chair is responsible for calling these sessions and using them appropriately, but any board member may request one. Bylaws or board policies determine how to proceed.

Chief executives sometimes feel threatened by closed meetings from which they are excluded. For example: A chief executive was distressed when she realized that the board was suddenly meeting alone and barred her, specifically, from the room. Afterwards it became clear that the board wanted to plan the details for a special anniversary in her honor. To ease unnecessary worries, the board must communicate with the chief executive following the session and inform him or her of possible conclusions or recommendations that surfaced during the meeting. If the board holds these meetings on a regular basis — for instance, before or after each board meeting — suspicions can be dispelled. Trust and regular open communication will alleviate apprehension.

Q Our chief executive tends to get a bit uptight about executive sessions. How can we clearly outline the situations when the board can and should meet alone without her — without creating any anxiety for her?

A As necessary as it is for the board to work closely with the chief executive, there are situations when the board needs to take a step aside and discuss issues alone. Some of these situations include

- Chief executive performance assessment. Board members need to be able to bring out issues in privacy and seek agreement with peers. The final "report" is what matters.

- Chief executive compensation. Compensation issues often are based on negotiations and both sides need to plan their own approach. The final figures naturally are shared with the chief executive and get reported on Form 990.

- Chief executive succession planning. Planning for the eventual change of guards is good governance. The board is responsible for making it happen efficiently with due diligence. Private discussions are warranted.

- Meeting with auditor. No staff should be present when the board communicates with the auditor about the details of the organization's financial management.

- Self-reflection. From time to time the board needs to have a moment to address its own performance issues in private — or simply let the guard down among peers.

The minutes of the board meeting should indicate when the board has met in executive session. There should be a record of the purpose of the session, time and place, who was present, and a description of any actions taken. Sometimes these notes are mere annotations because the session simply helped the board to prepare for open discussion on a tricky item. These records should be shared with any or all participants afterwards. Executive session minutes or notes are not shared with outsiders, as that would betray the meeting's confidentiality.

CONVENING AN ORGANIZATION'S MEMBERSHIP

Let's clarify terms first. A "member" can be very confusing and may have many different meanings:

- An organization may have a membership program that, for a fee, provides members with special benefits such as discounts, newsletters, or access to special Web site documents. In this context, the membership has no input into programmatic areas or the composition of the board — nor any other special affiliation with the nonprofit.

- A nonprofit may have members who are actually supporters of the mission and work of the organization. For instance, for a fee, members of a health-related organization may receive regular information on a particular illness, the latest research results, or suggestions for prevention and treatment. Again, the membership is not necessarily involved in the decisions that the board or the organization makes but members personally value its mission and work.

- A formal membership organization is one whose mission is to serve its members, such as a trade association, and one that invites its members to take an active role in the affairs of the nonprofit. The role of the members is outlined in the articles of incorporation and bylaws. Members usually elect the board and possibly also the officers of the board. They may also have the right to approve changes in the bylaws as well as major organizational decisions. Setting up a formal membership organization is a significant move and should not be taken lightly.

Any nonprofit that has a formal membership structure must also understand the legal rights of its members and for the membership's meetings. The source for these laws is the state nonprofit incorporation act. The Web site www.whpgs.org/f.htm can serve as a preliminary tool for research, but the office of the secretary of state or attorney general should also be able to provide the necessary information. State nonprofit associations also serve as an excellent reference for these issues.

Q **Can you suggest wording for our annual meeting invitation that would motivate members to attend?**

A The style of the invitation naturally depends on the culture of your organization but you will have a better attendance if your invitation discusses

- how members have a chance to influence the direction and future of their organization

- how voting is one of their benefits as members

- how their votes will enable the board to take the organization to the next level

- how they can influence the kinds of benefits that they will receive as members

Include an agenda. Highlight the importance of specific issues to be discussed. Address the individual, not the generic membership.

State laws normally explain the processes for certain voting procedures and for sending out membership meeting notices. If quorum requirements are not detailed in the organization's bylaws, state laws will usually define these requirements (a common members' quorum is a mere 10 percent of the voting membership, but considerable deviation from this example exists).

A membership organization's annual meeting is usually not as confusing as one in an organization with a self-perpetuating board. It is common to tie annual meetings to the organization's annual conference. Professional conferences are the attraction to get members to come together. Mere elections would not necessarily provide this motivation. In addition to attending conference activities, the membership also has the incentive of exercising its right to influence the internal affairs of the organization by electing a capable board and having an influence on the kinds of benefits offered by the organization.

Most state laws allow proxy voting in membership meetings. This makes sense, as it is often impossible in large member organizations to gather all or even the majority of members in the same room at the same time. Usually in addition to casting a vote at meeting, voting can be done by mail or electronically. Most member voting issues turn out to be simple yes or no votes on prestated issues, or choosing a candidate from a slate. (Please see sample proxies in Appendix VIII.) Communication with the membership prior to the meeting takes the role of deliberation of traditional board meetings, as proxy voting is a common method of participation. Membership meetings can also turn into heated debates, but in the end the objective is to reach a decision — particularly because reconvening the meeting at a later date can be costly and complex. If adequate and impartial information is shared with every voting member, it should be possible to conduct an unbiased election or receive a fair result of the members' opinion on an issue.

PROPER PROCEDURES FOR AN ELECTION MEETING

When ballots are used for voting at a membership meeting, a special election task force, or tellers, can ensure that proper process is respected. This committee or task force may have the following duties to ensure that the meeting structure is faultless:

- Ensure legality of the process.
- Determine who can vote.
- Validate proxies.
- Prepare and distribute ballots.
- Collect and validate ballots.
- Provide a tally of the votes.
- Announce the results.
- Prepare a report.

The bylaws should outline the chosen processes so that no one needs to inquire about state laws or wonder how and if a specific issue is covered. Additional details can be described in a policy manual, referencing membership meetings. Having an election committee in place ensures the reliability and trustworthiness of the voting process.

RETREATS: HELPING TO GO FORWARD

Board retreats constitute a very special type of meeting. In some ways, they could be considered as special meetings, but because their structure and purpose is so different from a meeting where organizational decisions are made, they warrant a category of their own.

Retreats involve the board as a group. They are often used for purposes of education, training, reflection, planning, or socializing. A retreat brings board members (and frequently senior staff) together in an environment where free communication and brainstorming is possible. Often an outside facilitator is brought in to lead the proceedings and give every board member the opportunity to participate fully. Retreats can last from several hours to several days, often taking place over a weekend. Besides business, socializing usually plays an important role during retreats. This is an excellent opportunity to mix work and recreation in order to allow board members to get to know one another more intimately in a setting different from the more formal boardroom.

A retreat can be organized around a board orientation, a strategic planning session, a fundraising workshop, a board self-assessment, or a discussion of major internal or external strategic issues that are important to the nonprofit. (Please see a sample agenda for an orientation retreat in Appendix IX.) If possible, the retreat should not take place in an office setting. A different environment helps send the message that new ideas and innovation are in order and creativity is desirable. There are a variety of special retreat accommodations to choose from, and the board can be creative in selecting the location. A board can plan a retreat on a cruise ship, around a hiking tour or music festival, or other relevant events that tie the mission of the organization to the board's focus. A good mixture of programmatic brainstorming activities and entertainment can help board members leave the retreat with a personal and professional sense of satisfaction and accomplishment.

TIP

During the next retreat, try one of the following ways to help the board generate ideas, brainstorm solutions, or address important issues.

Flipchart brainstorming — Using a flipchart, a large piece of butcher paper, or a chalk board, ask the board to generate a free-flowing list of ideas without censorship. Encourage freedom of thought, and do not discuss suggestions as they are presented. Save the discussion until the end of the exercise.

Fishbone — This exercise is used to analyze cause and effect. On a large piece of paper, draw the head and the bones of a fish. Next to the head write down a problem. Label the backbone with a possible cause. As other causes surface add those to the side bones.

Mind mapping — Draw a circle on a big piece of paper and write a word inside, representing an issue. Draw lines off of the circle and label them with the various aspects of the issue. Add new lines with relating ideas as spokes off the main lines.

Sticky notes — Ask each board member to write down individual ideas on separate pieces of sticky note paper and place them on the wall or in the middle of a table. Together, the board separates all ideas into similar categories and discusses the results.

Subgroups — Divide the group into smaller subgroups and ask each team to discuss either the same issue or separate issues and record their suggestions. Have a leader from each group present their findings to the main group.

Because of the nature of the meeting, retreats are rarely structured as normal board meetings. However, a retreat needs careful planning in order to ensure its success. It often makes sense to involve board members in retreat planning and organization. With ownership comes commitment. Retreats should be scheduled well ahead of time as busy board members need to manage their calendars, and travel and hotel accommodations may be involved. Spouses accompanying board members should be included in any social activities. The business side of the retreat, however, should not be open to family or friends.

TIP

To plan a successful board retreat take the following actions:

- Get the chair on board to serve as the inspiration and meet the leadership challenges of the role.

- Schedule the retreat well ahead of time to allow board members to put it in their calendars.

- Get a commitment from all members to attend. Attending a retreat is as important as attending a regular board meeting.

- Give board members "homework" ahead of time to prepare them for fruitful discussion.

- Set clear goals. There is a purpose for the retreat.

- Meet outside of the normal boardroom setting.

- Have plenty of free time to allow socializing and even special programs.

- Set a relaxed tone for the meeting: casual dress, icebreakers, fewer structural rules, flexibility.

- Leave voting for the subsequent regular meeting.

Follow up your action plan!

The deliverables of a retreat depend on the purpose of the meeting. If the purpose is to discuss the results of a self-assessment, the board should produce an outline for future actions. A retreat focusing on strategic planning should include someone responsible for drafting the final document or taking the next steps. And the results of a retreat centered on better understanding of board members' roles and responsibilities will hopefully be evident at subsequent board meetings.

REMEMBER

- Vary your meeting makeup! Board work does not happen only in a pre-scheduled and structured meeting. Work gets accomplished in many types of meetings and they all require board members' attention.

- Whether you convene your board's first session, organize an annual meeting for the board or the members, invite committee members to work together, head to a retreat, or reorganize your personal affairs to be present in an impromptu emergency meeting, make sure you are prepared and understand the protocol to accomplish the task.

CASE STUDY
TWO (OR THREE OR FOUR) HEADS ARE BETTER THAN ONE

The PQR board wanted to learn more about the Sarbanes-Oxley Act and asked its governance committee to assemble and present a roster of leadership development activities addressing the Act. Travis, the committee chair, told the committee members that he would contact them to set up a conference call to discuss next steps. One week stretched to two and then three. When Travis finally called, the only time all of the members could meet was a week before the upcoming board meeting, which was cutting it close.

When the committee members finally met, Travis started out by saying, "Good news — I've completed the roster, and I've got the speakers all lined up." He told the committee that there really wasn't any point to having a lengthy call and promised to e-mail the members the roster before the board meeting. He did, the day of the meeting. When it came time to present the information, Travis did so without including the other committee members. Unfortunately, it appeared that Travis didn't really understand the Sarbanes-Oxley Act. Fundraising was on the schedule but document retention and destruction was not!

When a board member refuses to gather team insight, his or her board work will lack a diversity of knowledge and opinion. The board member might also end up wasting his or her own time if the rest of the board decides to redo the work as a team. The PQR board chair and board might address the current situation by taking one of the following steps:

- Talk to Travis about the importance and value of involving others in committee work; after all, isn't that the point of having a committee? Why set up a working group if not everyone will be involved in discussing the issues and deciding what recommendations to take to the board? Travis and the board would have benefited from the input of the other committee members to ensure that the roster was complete and on topic.

- Remind Travis that, as the chair of the committee, it is his responsibility to ensure that committee meetings take place. He is the facilitator of the group and needs to determine the best communications methods between the committee members.

- Train all board members on committee responsibility. Were any staff members considered to support the committee efforts? Did the committee members speak up when they hadn't heard anything from Travis? All board members, committee members or not, should be holding each other accountable for their work. A formal process should be put in place for electing committee chairs and for conducting regular evaluations regarding the need for committees and the work of the committee members.

Adapted from *Taming the Troublesome Board Member* by Katha Kissman, BoardSource, 2006.

CONCLUSION

There are as many distinctive boards as there are organizations — each one of them excelling and struggling with different issues with different means and success. And so it goes with board meetings. There is no sense in drafting step-by-step strict rules on how a board should operate during its meetings. Each board must find this through its own trial and error.

This book provides boards with options for contemplation. The best advice for running a meeting is to use common sense, know the legal framework, and be guided by the board's expectations. Design the processes and operating framework accordingly as they fit the board's culture, and simply act like reasonable adults with good will and passion.

If there are any messages to take away from this guide, remember the following three objectives: *Be flexible. Define the boundaries. Make meetings matter.*

It is the board that determines what works best. A board must work collectively, learn from each other, and teach each other — no matter how different the players are. Each board must figure out what processes bring the desired outcomes and then be brave enough to follow through, even if the means do not correspond to the traditional norms. Each board member must keep an open mind while adapting to team culture. Individuality is an asset in a board member, but it's the collective body that determines the course of action.

Flexibility does not imply that there are no boundaries. Board meetings must follow legal conventions, bylaws stipulations, ethical guidelines, and rules and protocol that define civil and considerate behavior. When members do not know what is acceptable, they can step out of line and compromise their intentions. Knowing the limitations eliminates ambiguity and provides fairness and integrity to the processes.

If board meetings do not focus on real, important, and relevant issues, they can be a waste of time. No matter how impeccable and considerate the processes are, if the board is working on the wrong issues, it is only perfecting the outer framework. The purpose of the board meeting is to bring board members together to steer the organization to its next level of potential. If the meeting time is spent on trivial issues, members will lose interest and feel unappreciated. Being strategic in planning the meetings' focus allows the board to stay one step ahead, be proactive, and productively advance the mission of the organization.

So, how do you detect a successful board meeting? When the meeting is over, board members walk out, chatting with each other — even smiling — because they feel they added value, their decisions will push the organization forward, and ultimately there will be concrete results among those served by the organization. A good meeting is a meeting of minds that are able to rely on the collective wisdom.

As much as this book focuses on group dynamics and flexibility of process, it is important to stress that certain ground rules have their place in the boardroom. Even laid-back meetings must remain legal and orderly. Order in the boardroom does not prohibit a friendly, congenial, or even relaxed atmosphere. Ground rules can eliminate irregularities and the unfair treatment of some board members. Like with any protocol, ground rules take away ambiguity, embarrassment, and missteps in unclear situations. Below is a list of some of the key elements that can provide structure to your meetings without turning them into sessions where process trumps performance.

1. **Civility** — Start with politeness, professionalism, and respect for others. This is simple adult behavior that is the expected norm in every board meeting.

2. **Chair** — If your meeting does not have someone chairing it, you will have a group of individuals managing themselves. Just try dealing with the cacophony that happens when everybody in the room is determined to make their point all at once! A skillful and unbiased facilitator manages the process, participants, and atmosphere.

3. **Quorum** — The very first thing the board must do before starting its meeting is ask the presiding officer or the secretary to determine whether you have enough qualified voting members present. If you do not have a quorum, the only practical decision you can make is to adjourn the meeting and determine when to continue.

4. **Call to Order** — Every board meeting starts with a call to order. That is the official opening of the session when the business of the meeting begins. Whether you use the customary "The meeting will come to order" or another more colloquial phrase ultimately does not matter. Any discussion or decision is now part of the order of the meeting and the results will be recorded in the minutes. If you do not have an official start, you may have difficulties getting everybody's attention and, afterwards, you may wonder whether an issue was part of the meeting.

4. **Motions** — When we talk about parliamentary order, we often erroneously equate that term with motions. Even if your board does not follow strict parliamentary rules — and there are arguments why that is not necessarily the best approach for many small nonprofit boards — relying on motions to present issues for consideration makes sense. A motion basically is a structured way of bringing up a point that you want the board to address. The chair has to grant you permission to speak, you say "I move that…," and state your proposal. Some complicated motions can be presented in a written resolution format ("Resolved, that…") but you still have to introduce them to the rest of the board. Using motions sets a tone for a business meeting where issues are introduced in an orderly fashion.

5. **Seconding** — If you introduce a motion, you will also need to have that motion seconded. This simply means that a peer will say "Second!" and indicate that your suggestion is valid for deliberation. If nobody speaks (you do not need permission for this quick exclamation) even after the chair invites you to do so, this motion is dead and will not be considered.

6. **Deliberation** — Under most circumstances, it is impossible and imprudent to jump from seconding to voting. The major part of your meeting time should be spent on discussion, debate, argument, counterargument, and justifying opinions. These sections of the meeting are the bread-and-butter parts. Use them liberally and wisely.

7. **Abstentions** — During the voting phase, some members will vote for and against while others will decide that their only option is to abstain. Whatever the motivation, it means that this board member does not want to express his or her opinion on that particular issue. If there is no conflict of interest involved, a person abstaining needs to realize that his or her nonvote may prevent the majority from carrying the vote. An abstention may end up counting as a negative vote.

8. **Adjournment** — A meeting starts with a call to order and ends with adjournment. By closing the meeting the chair indicates that all motions have been completed and that official business has been accomplished. The chair may simply say, "If there are no objections, the meeting will adjourn."

9. **Minutes** — Recording the minutes of a meeting cannot be avoided. You may have a secretary of the board do this, or, as is also common, assign a staff member to handle this task. The board has no choice in whether the minutes are kept, so keep them as clear, comprehensible, and unambiguous as possible.

10. **Follow Up** — Thank participants. Remind them of their promises. Get ready for the next meeting.

Structure, when not overbearing, can sometimes bring freedom. Neither you nor your board members need to constantly worry about procedures but can focus on the purpose of the meeting: You are here to help your organization do exceptional things!

The pain of parting is nothing to the joy of meeting again.
— Charles Dickens

APPENDIX I
SAMPLE MEETING AGENDAS

SAMPLE 1

[Name of organization]
Board of Directors Meeting
Monday, September 15, 20XX 8:30 a.m. – 4:30 p.m.
2000 Main Street, Suite 200
Our Town, VA 22222

A. Welcome and Chair's Remarks

B. Consent Agenda

- Approval of minutes of June 15, 20XX

- Approval of Agenda

- Chief Executive's Report

- Treasurer's Report

- Committee Reports

C. Collaboration Proposal

D. Introduction to New Membership Program

E. Upcoming Planning Process

F. Adjournment

SAMPLE 2

[Name of organization]
Board of Directors Meeting
Date: Monday, March 15, 20XX
Time: 6:00 p.m.
Location: 100 Main Street, Our Town, ME 01234

Agenda Items	Accountable	Purpose	Time
Welcome	Chair		5 min.
Introduction of new members	Chair	Information	5 min.
Consent Agenda • Previous minutes • President's report • Committee reports • Leasing contract	Chair	Decision	1 min.
City contract proposal	John Murphy	Decision	15 min.
Summer program	Dianne Letts	Decision	15 min.
Relocation proposal	Cary Mann	Discussion	30 min.
Term limits	Becky Lowes	Discussion	20 min.
Adjournment	Chair		1 min.

APPENDIX II
SAMPLE CONTENTS OF A BOARD BOOK

Board books should reach board members at least one week before the meeting. Their purpose is to allow board members to prepare properly for the meeting and to feel comfortable with the consent agenda items. The book should/could contain

- Agenda
- Consent agenda clearly noted
- Financial statements
- President's report
- Committee reports
- Any relevant background information for discussion items
- Update on the issues to be voted on
- Related newspaper articles
- Update on relevant legal issues affecting the organization
- Organization's newsletter

APPENDIX III
SAMPLE MINUTES TEMPLATES

SAMPLE 1

[Name of organization]
Board of Directors Meeting
Minutes of [date]

The Board of Directors of [name of organization] met on [date, time, place].

Attendance
Members present:
Members absent:
Staff present:
Guests:

A. Consent agenda
[Indicate if any of the items were removed from the consent agenda.]

Action:

B. Issue

Outline of discussion

Action:

C. Issue

Outline of discussion

Action:

D. Issue

Outline of discussion

Action:

Attachments

SAMPLE 2

Board of Directors Meeting Minutes
[Name and address of the organization]
[Time and place of the meeting]
Present:
Absent:

Item	Board Member	Action
Welcoming remarks	Liam Smith, chair	called meeting to order
	Liam Smith, chair	introduced new members [names]
	Lilly Hitton	moved consent agenda to be approved
	Mark Jones	seconded
City contract proposal	John Murphy	outlined the proposal (see attachment)
	Kerry Shannon	moved to approve the contract
	Mark Jones	seconded the motion
	Dianne Letts	objected due to reporting constraints
	Full board	voted, motion passed

Item	Board Member	Action
Summer program	Dianne Letts	introduced advanced plans for summer camp (see attachment)
	Tina Jeffries	moved to approve the plan
	Will Blass	seconded
	Full board	voted, motion passed
Relocation proposal	Cary Mann	explained the need for relocation due to poor condition of the present building
	Denice Johnston	requested the formation of a task force to look into pros and cons
	Tina Davies	seconded
	Full board	agreed to elect a task force; Lisa Letts requested a report for the next meeting
	Becky Lowes	outlined the present term limit structure of the board; suggested formation of a task force to study benchmark data
	Dina Davies	seconded
	Full board	agreed to appoint a task force; Dina Davies requested a report for the next meeting
	Denice Johnston	seconded
Adjournment	Liam Smith, chair	adjourned the meeting at 7:45 p.m.

APPENDIX IV
SAMPLE COMMITTEE REPORT TEMPLATE

Date:
Committee:
Members present:
Type of report:

- Update

- Recommendation for board action

- Recommendation for a policy change

Outline of issues:

Background information/support materials:

Recommendation:

APPENDIX V
SAMPLE BALLOTS

SAMPLE 1 BALLOT FOR ELECTION OF BOARD TREASURER

Instructions: Vote for three candidates. Mark preferences by using 1 or 2, with 1 indicating your first choice. Do not give any tie votes. The candidate with the highest score is the next treasurer.

Candidates	Rating
David Anderson	
Christy Bowman	
Bertha Cooper	
Alvin Dotson	

SAMPLE 2 BALLOT FOR OFFICER ELECTIONS

Instructions: To vote, place an "X" in the square beside the name of the candidate of your choice.

Chair

- ❏ Mike Diller
- ❏ Mary Harvin

Treasurer

- ❏ Paula Barker
- ❏ Laura Piper

APPENDIX VI
SAMPLE RESOLUTIONS

SAMPLE 1

Resolution for Relocating the Office

Resolved, that the headquarters of [name of organization] will be relocated to Peoria, Kansas, in June 20XX.

SAMPLE 2

Resolution to Recognize the Service of a Long-Time Board Member [Format this document as a letter.]

Larry Michaels, you are a respected colleague and a valued friend. After more than a decade of service with us, we offer our profound thanks for your steadfast commitment to [name of organization] and your participation as a member of this board.

This resolution is passed by unanimous acclamation and entered into the official minutes of today's meeting of the board of directors.

APPENDIX VII
SAMPLE MEETING EVALUATIONS

SAMPLE 1

MEETING ASSESSMENT

Issue	Yes	No	Suggestions
Meeting followed the agenda			
Agenda focused on future issues			
Meeting started and ended on time			
All board members were active participants			
Chair led the meeting with skill			

SAMPLE 2

MEETING ASSESSMENT

Please comment if you do not agree with the following statements:

- Board book materials helped me prepare for this meeting.
- Our meeting focused on the right issues that should be our board's concern.
- We stayed on track and kept the mission as our guide.
- We covered all the issues thoroughly and objectively.
- I left the meeting knowing what I need to do next.

My additional suggestions to improve our board meetings:

SAMPLE 3

KEY QUESTIONS ABOUT MEETINGS

The following are some key questions designed to help board and staff prepare for board meetings and to focus on the right issues before, during, and after the meeting. These questions — appropriately framed to address an individual and to take into account the culture of the board — could be incorporated into meeting evaluations and/or board self-assessments.

Before the meeting

- Are board members receiving board books well in advance?

- Have board members read the material and provided appropriate feedback? Do they understand and agree with the inclusion of the issues in the agenda?

- Is the material presented in a concise and focused manner? Is it easy to understand the main points of the agenda or do the main points get buried in trivia?

During the meeting

- Is the chair an effective meeting facilitator?

- Is there something new and surprising happening at every meeting?

- Is the discussion focusing on the big issues or are debates about administrative and management-related details?

- Do board members feel well utilized and that they are able to contribute their skills and expertise?

- Do board members leave feeling as though they have learned something?

- Are board members respectful of the comments and contributions of fellow members?

- Are members in basic agreement of the main issues even if their approach may be different?

- Are meetings always in the same old boring place with the same old boring food?

After the meeting

- Did anything happen between the last meeting and the next one?

- Do board members feel as though they have wasted their time and nothing got accomplished?

- Did board members actually finish their tasks before the next meeting?

- Is anyone communicating with board members in between the meetings?

Other underlying issues

- Are board members genuinely interested in the mission of the organization?
- Are members worn out and tired of the commitment?
- Do members make wholehearted efforts to participate and collaborate?
- Do members come to every board meeting?
- Do members demonstrate an understanding of the issues?

APPENDIX VIII
SAMPLE PROXY

The undersigned appoints _____ as my proxy to vote on my behalf on board elections at the Annual Meeting of [name of association], on February 28, 20XX.

Signature

February 1, 20XX

APPENDIX IX
SAMPLE AGENDA FOR AN ORIENTATION RETREAT

Location: Red Roof Hotel Conference Facilities

Time: January 15, 20XX, 9:00 a.m. – 8:30 p.m.

Objectives: To introduce new board members to the organization, fellow board members, and our board processes

9:00 a.m.   Breakfast

9:30   Welcoming remarks
             Introductions of board members, chief executive, facilitator
             Introduction to the organization
             Questions and answers

10:15   Presentation on board member responsibilities and role of the board
             Clarification of expectations
             Small group discussion

12:00 p.m.   Lunch

1:00   Introduction to teamwork; role playing

2:30   Coffee break

3:00   Presentation of board processes and structure
             Group discussion on how to share work

4:00   Fundraising challenges

4:30   Wrap-up
             Sharing of first impressions

5:00   Free time

6:00   Gathering at the lobby for drinks and dinner

Guest speaker: How to make your board experience exciting

GLOSSARY

Abstention: Not casting a vote because of conflict of interest or ignorance of the matter at hand

Adjourn: To motion to officially close a meeting

Adopt: To approve or accept a motion by voting

Agenda: A list of issues to be discussed in a meeting, including order of business

Amend: To modify or change the wording of a motion before it is voted on

Annual meeting: [Usually] a legally required meeting where new board members and officers are elected

Ballot: A blank piece of paper or a form used in secret voting

Board book: Materials, including the agenda, that board members need to receive to prepare for the meeting

Call to Order: An official opening of a meeting

Carry: To adopt or approve a motion

Chair: The presiding officer during a board meeting

Conflict of interest: A personal or professional interest that prevents a board member from making an unbiased decision

Consensus: An agreement that all participants can accept by eliminating objections

Consent agenda: A portion of a meeting agenda where routine items are listed and voted on together without further discussion

Decorum: Appropriateness of conduct in meetings

Deliberation: A process of careful consideration and debate of issues to be voted on during a meeting

Election committee: A committee responsible for the voting process (usually) during a membership meeting

Executive committee: A standing board committee that usually has the power to act on behalf of the board

Executive session: A closed segment of a meeting of the board where usually no staff is present

Ex officio: By virtue of the office; refers to members who serve on the board because of the position they hold; voting rights must be specified separately

Icebreaker: A facilitation exercise in the beginning of a meeting to start with a good team spirit

KPAWN meeting: A meeting between the board and the chief executive where the chief executive may openly discuss issues that "keep the president awake at night"

Majority: More than half of the votes cast

Minutes: A legal record of the actions during a meeting

Motion: A formal proposal for action during a meeting

Notice of meeting: A message, usually written, to clarify the date and the place of the meeting, sent to every member who has the right to attend the meeting

Parliamentary order: Rules and procedures for deliberative assemblies

Poll: A census or survey method for voters to express their opinion

Private agenda: Personal motivation and interest guiding decision making

Pro tem: For the time being; refers to a temporary chair of a meeting

Proxy: Authorization of a person to vote or act on someone's behalf

Quorum: The minimum number of members required present before business can be carried out

Rescind: To cancel a previous decision

Resolution: A formal, longer or often more complicated motion presented in a written format for board action; a resolution is "resolved" rather than "moved"

Retreat: A brainstorming or an action-oriented meeting

Robert's Rules of Order: The leading manual of parliamentary order

Roll call: Determination of who is present by reading the names of the members aloud

Rules of order: Written parliamentary rules that guide the meeting process

Second: An approval of a motion by another member during a meeting

Secondary motions: Related motions that can be made while the primary motion is still pending

Secretary: The board officer traditionally responsible for keeping the minutes

Sunshine laws: State open meeting laws

Tellers: Persons appointed or elected to count the votes and to report to the assembly

Unanimous vote: There are no dissenting votes among those who voted on the issue

Vice chair: The board officer who usually chairs the meeting when the chair is not available

Voice vote: A voting method for board members to indicate "yes" or "no"

Vote: A formal expression of an opinion under consideration

SUGGESTED RESOURCES

Angelica, Marion Peters. *Resolving Conflict in Nonprofit Organizations.* St. Paul, MN: Fieldstone Alliance, 1999. The guide's eight-step process shows you how to spot conflicts, decide whether to intervene, uncover and deal with the true issues involved, and design and carry out a conflict-resolution process. Helpful worksheets, checklists, and conflict-resolution forms keep the process on track, with additional exercises for learning and practicing conflict-resolution skills.

Axelrod, Nancy R. *Culture of Inquiry: Healthy Debate in the Boardroom.* Washington, DC: BoardSource, 2007. This book explains how to create a culture of inquiry within the boardroom — one marked by mutual respect and constructive debate that leads to sound and shared decision making.

BoardSource Committee Series. Six books. Washington, DC: BoardSource, 2004. This series features an introductory publication, *Transforming Board Structure: Strategies for Committees and Task Forces,* that provides a fresh look at how boards can streamline the work of the full board. Included is a CD-ROM with customizable tools and worksheets that are helpful in job descriptions, interview questions, and policies appropriate to specific committees. Also included in the series are the following books: *Governance Committee, Executive Committee, Financial Committees, Development Committee, and Advisory Councils.* Learn about the most crucial committees of the board and how each committee is unique in operation and intent.

BoardSource. *The Nonprofit Board Answer Book: A Practical Guide for Board Members and Chief Executives, Second Edition.* San Francisco, CA: Jossey-Bass. This *Answer Book* is organized in an easy-to-follow question-and-answer format and covers almost every situation you're likely to encounter in nonprofit board governance, from structuring a board for success to conducting productive meetings. Also included are reminders at the end of the chapters, real-life examples, case studies, and worksheets.

Ernstthal, Henry L. "Deciding How to Decide." *Association Management* (Vol. 54), March 2002. Henry Ernstthal has developed a process to help determine who is supposed to be engaged in decision making within the nonprofit. This process can help veer off micromanagement as it guides appropriate issues away from the board and into the hands of the staff. A predetermined process of deciding how to decide can eliminate unnecessary friction among the various parties and avoid unilateral action.

Hopkins, Bruce R. *Legal Responsibilities of Nonprofit Boards, Second Edition.* Washington, DC: BoardSource, 2009. All board members should understand their legal responsibilities, including when and how they can be held personally liable and what type of oversight they should provide. Discover the essential information that board members should know to protect themselves and their organization. Written in nontechnical language, this book provides legal concepts and definitions, as well as a detailed discussion on ethics.

Horton, Thomas R. "Groupthink in the Boardroom." *Directors & Boards,* Winter 2002. Tom Horton contemplates the mystery of how being part of a group of cohorts can dim your individual thinking and take you with the crowd without posing pertinent questions. His thought: "Good boards encourage both coherence and dissent."

Hughes, Sandra R. *To Go Forward, Retreat! The Board Retreat Handbook.* E-book. Washington, DC: BoardSource, 1999. A board retreat is perhaps the best place to address some of an organization's challenging issues. Whether you are planning a retreat around board orientation, strategic planning, or board self-assessment, this book provides dos and don'ts of successful retreat planning. The text includes tips for icebreakers, seating arrangements, involving staff and guests, and getting input from participants in the planning process. Also included are a retreat checklist and pre-retreat planning questionnaires.

Ingram, Richard T. *Ten Basic Responsibilities of Nonprofit Boards, Second Edition.* Washington, DC: BoardSource, 2009. More than 200,000 board members have already discovered this #1 BoardSource bestseller. This newly revised edition explores the 10 core areas of board responsibility. Share with board members the basic responsibilities, including determining mission and purpose, ensuring effective planning, and participating in fundraising. You'll find that this is an ideal reference for drafting job descriptions, assessing board performance, and orienting board members on their responsibilities.

Katzenbach, Jon R., and Douglas K. Smith. "The Discipline of Virtual Teams." *Leader to Leader,* Fall 2001. This article studies how making virtual teams affects the teams' performance. Surprisingly, the authors conclude that technology as a tool is not the critical factor in performance — undisciplined behavior is. At the end, the authors recommend face-to-face sessions for problem solving and virtual meetings for information sharing and updates.

Kelsey, Dee, and Pam Plumb. *Great Meetings! How to Facilitate Like a Pro.* Portland, ME: Hanson Park Press, 2001. *Great Meetings!* addresses challenges of meeting facilitation and provides practical tools, outlines, checklists, and options for handling group interaction and problem situations in the most productive manner possible. A facilitator will learn how to handle conflicts and when to intervene to make the best out of a tense situation.

McLaughlin, Thomas A. "Time to Work: No More Monthly Board Meetings." *NonProfit Times,* October 1, 2001. How often a board needs to meet depends on the amount of work to be accomplished. Too-frequent meetings tend to encourage short-term thinking rather than enhance the board's supervisory capacity. A decision to meet less frequently should not happen in a vacuum, but careful analysis will help the board find the optimal number of meetings per year.

Orlikoff, James E., and Mary K. Totten. "Trustee Workbook: How to Run Effective Board Meetings." *Trustee,* April 2001. This article focuses on the main elements of effective meetings: keeping the board as the decision-making body, avoiding trivia in the agendas, ensuring the meetings are regularly evaluated for their efficiency, and bringing the right people into the boardroom.

Peterson, Mary. "Constructive Conflict." *Association Management,* August 2002. Conflict is a natural phenomenon; how we deal with it turns it into a negative or positive exchange. Peterson addresses honesty as one of the essential ingredients of conflict management. We also need to examine existing — written and unwritten — agreements between various participants to clarify expectations, she says. Actively dealing with conflict rather than avoiding it helps to keep the situation under control and not allow it to escalate into a major confrontation.

Pointer, Dennis, and James E. Orlikoff. *The High-Performance Board: Principles of Nonprofit Organization Governance.* San Francisco: Jossey-Bass, 2002. Sixty-four principles outline the critical areas that the board must pay attention to. The authors provide recommendations for each aspect of board focus and develop an action plan for continuous board education.

Robinson, Maureen. *Nonprofit Boards That Work.* New York: John Wiley & Sons, 2001. Maureen Robinson acknowledges that there is no unique formula that meets the needs of every board. The board's desire to do the best for the organization takes many forms. There is a solution to every situation and the author provokes each board to find its own application. The board must assume flexibility and adaptability to become a board that works.

Schwarz, Roger M. *The Skilled Facilitator: Practical Wisdom for Developing Effective Groups.* San Francisco: Jossey-Bass, 1994. A professional facilitator finds this book as the authoritative guide to ground rules of group interaction, proven techniques for starting a meeting and keeping it focused, practical methods for dealing with emotions that hinder progress, and a diagnostic tool to identifying problem areas.

Sunshine laws: www.rcfp.org/tapping/index.cgi. This Web site provides direct access to the various state sunshine laws.

Susskind, Lawrence, Sarah McKearnan, and Jennifer Thomas-Larmer. *The Consensus Building Handbook.* Thousand Oaks, CA: Sage Publications, 1999. Here is the most comprehensive resource on consensus building. Over 1,100 pages explain and document best practices in the consensus-building discipline. Experts in the field outline their methods to solve problems and make decisions in a group setting, and 17 case studies demonstrate how facilitators and mediators have relied on consensus-building principles.

Waldenmayer, Corinne. "Connecting a Far-flung Board." *Grantsmanship Center Magazine,* Fall 2002. National and international boards often struggle with distance-related obstacles to bring all board members together under the same roof. Technology-based tools connect remote regions and enable these boards to function. This article introduces options and helps organizations decide which ones are worth the investment.

Wertheimer, Mindy R. *The Board Chair Handbook, Second Edition.* Washington, DC: BoardSource, 2007. This handbook provides a complete guide to the chair's roles and responsibilities, suggestions for developing board policies and procedures, recommendations for handling a variety of problems, and advice for cultivating talent for future board leadership. Also included is a CD-ROM containing sample meeting agendas and customizable letters for asking a board member for a gift, cultivating and recruiting prospective board members, inviting someone to join the board, and more.

Zander, Alvin. *Making Boards Effective: The Dynamics of Nonprofit Governing Boards.* San Francisco: Jossey-Bass, 1993. This hardcover book remains the classic resource on interpersonal dynamics of boards. It tells a valid story of how individual board members' characteristics and the processes that the board chooses to employ affect the overall performance of the board. Understanding causes and effects of human behavior and the absence of committed decision making can lead to self-serving and rubber-stamping boards.

REFERENCES ON PARLIAMENTARY ORDER

Cochran, Alice Collier. *Roberta's Rules of Order: Sail Through Meetings with Stellar Results Without the Gavel.* San Francisco: Jossey-Bass, 2004. This guide introduces ultimate flexibility to board procedures. It advocates that each board creates its own meeting guidelines that best fit the board's culture and embrace democratic principles. Other features include introducing motions after the problem and possible solutions have been identified and using of concordance — substantial agreement — rather than majority rule or consensus.

Jenning, C. Alan. *Robert's Rules for Dummies.* New York: John Wiley and Sons, 2005. Here you have the parliamentary rules explained in a rather straightforward manner.

Keesey, Ray E. *Modern Parliamentary Procedure.* Washington, D.C.: American Psychological Association, 1994. 143 pages. Keesey's method was originally created for the American Psychological Association. It is a simplified system promoting open participation and deliberation. A reduced order and structure guides the meeting.

www.parliamentarians.org
The Web site of the National Association of Parliamentarians provides guidance and resources on meeting procedures.

www.parliamentaryprocedure.org
The Web site of the American Institute of Parliamentarians includes documents on parliamentary issues and book references on parliamentary order.

Robert's Rules of Order, Newly Revised, 10th Edition. Cambridge, MA: De Capo Press, 2000. With over 700 pages of parliamentary order, this is the most widely used handbook on meeting procedures. It dissects meetings into most minute regulations and provides an answer to all questions concerning proper parliamentary order. Provides formality to meetings but can be used to solve disagreements during more informal meetings as well.

Sturgis, Alice F. *Standard Code of Parliamentary Procedure.* New York, NY: McGraw Hill, 2000. This updated guide resembles Robert's Rules of Order but is simpler to use for smaller nonprofits.

Tortorice, Donald A. *The Modern Rules of Order.* Chicago, IL: American Bar Association, 2007. This guidebook provides a modern, simplified procedure for meetings that promotes efficiency, decorum, and fairness within an easily adopted format. It is best suited for meetings where members focus more on content than procedure.

ABOUT THE AUTHOR

Outi Flynn joined BoardSource in 1989 and today, as the director of the Knowledge Center, acts as one of BoardSource's key governance experts. She has developed, structured, and managed BoardSource's *Ask a Question* service and, in that capacity, has handled tens of thousands of governance and general nonprofit questions from BoardSource customers and staff. Remaining at the helm of this service has allowed her to stay abreast of cutting-edge issues of concern to the nonprofit sector.

In addition, Flynn has created and contributed to the bulk of the governance information available on BoardSource's Web site, including topic papers, white papers, and frequently asked questions, and she acts as the primary content reviewer for the organization's publications. She has also authored, co-authored, and contributed to several of BoardSource's publications.

Her areas of expertise range from fluency with overall sector issues, concerns, and dilemmas that plague nonprofit leaders on a daily basis to creative solutions for board members and chief executives who are struggling with structural and procedural challenges.